MADE
IN
INDIA

From the days of the Licence Raj, India has come a long way. This book is a fascinating account of the journey traversed by Indian enterprise. Sharply written, well researched, thought provoking and deftly crafted, this book is an exciting read for entrepreneurs, students and policymakers alike.

—N. Chandrasekaran,
Executive Chairman, Tata Sons

Amitabh Kant brings the interplay of policy, technology and innovation to life in an engaging manner. It is a rich and comprehensive account of the evolution of India's manufacturing industry. Succinct and easy to read, this book is an absorbing chronicle of how technologies are disrupting and reshaping industries in India, from mobility to renewable energy to healthcare.

—Anand Mahindra,
Chairman, Mahindra Group

Amitabh has written a fascinating chronicle of the recent history of India's private enterprise. This book demonstrates how economic policy can either thwart private enterprise or let it flourish. It is an insider's perspective, from a person who has passionately driven ease of doing business, innovation and technological change in government. The book presents a compelling and pragmatic perspective for the private sector to propel India to greater heights. His passion for India, its growth and progress shines through in every page! In many ways, the book inspires the reader to become a change agent as we advance towards India@100.

—Nandan Nilekani,
Chairman and Co-Founder, Infosys
and Founding Chairman, UIDAI (Aadhaar)

Amitabh Kant's account of the history of India's private enterprise is a must-read for all those who are passionate about India's manufacturing and start-up story. This book is an excellent account of how India's enterprises, once laggards at the world stage, are among the most competitive now. It captures beautifully how India's start-ups are leading this charge and how this innovative spirit has to be further unleashed as India accelerates the pace of growth. Kant is someone who has been at the heart of India's industrial policy thinking for over two decades and is in a position to offer unique perspectives on the subject.

—**Sanjeev Bikhchandani,**
Co-Founder, Info Edge

MADE
IN
INDIA

75 YEARS OF BUSINESS AND ENTERPRISE

AMITABH KANT

RUPA

Published by
Rupa Publications India Pvt. Ltd 2023
7/16, Ansari Road, Daryaganj
New Delhi 110002

Sales centres:
Prayagraj Bengaluru Chennai
Hyderabad Jaipur Kathmandu
Kolkata Mumbai

P-ISBN: 978-93-5702-068-8
E-ISBN: 978-93-5702-075-6

Third impression 2023

10 9 8 7 6 5 4 3

The moral right of the author has been asserted.

Printed in India

CONTENTS

INTRODUCTION

LOOKING BACK
TO MARCH AHEAD

As India completes 75 years of Independence, we have seen much change. The Indian economy now stands as among the largest and fastest growing in the world, truly breaking free from the shackles of colonialism. Recently, India overtook the UK to become the world's fifth-biggest economy. India's rise to the heights of the global economy is merely a return to where it was on the eve of colonization. However, it was not the policies instituted post-Independence that were responsible for India's standing in the global economy today. One of the biggest differences between now and 1947 is the role of private enterprise. Kept on the peripheries of the economy by design, private enterprise is now driving India's growth story. This evolution is the central theme of this book, which traces the genesis of India's private enterprise since the pre-Independence era to modern times.

Once a leader in the global economy, centuries of colonization saw India being deindustrialized and falling behind. Indian entrepreneurs reignited India's industrialization efforts in the late colonial era, but India moved 'From British Raj to Licence Raj' after Independence in 1947. This chapter attempts to understand why that happened. It presents and analyses the post-Independence policies and their impact on private enterprise. In today's environment where allusions to the 'Licence Raj' are made in response to policy initiatives, it is important to understand what the Licence Raj truly meant and represented. It was not merely a web of rules and regulations that shackled private enterprise. The chapter will help readers better understand the policies of that time and the implications of a command-and-control economy.

As the years progressed, it became increasingly clear that the model India was following was not working. Inefficiency and rent-seeking became the hallmarks of the economy as we teetered from one foreign exchange crisis to another. Cracks were papered over, and rather than looking outwards, we continued to look inwards. By the time the crisis of the 1990s hit, the cracks had become gaping wide. Systemic change was needed.

In the early 1990s, a complete reorientation of policies placed India on the path to becoming a global player again. The chapter 'Tryst with Reforms' chronicles the economic reforms of the 1990s, before presenting their impact. The effect of economic liberalization was clear. After a period of deindustrialization, it was the Indian entrepreneur that led India's reindustrialization. New industries boomed and new career paths came to the fore. A new kind of entrepreneur built the behemoths of today. Soon, Indian companies not just entered but also thrived on the global stage.

After years of 'golden growth', the global financial crisis derailed India's growth story. The reform agenda had run of out steam as well. India, despite opening its economy, remained one of the hardest places to do business in. Global confidence in India's economy was faltering. Foreign investment started to dry up. A new paradigm had to be ushered in to restore domestic and global faith in the economy.

The new paradigm of 2014 saw a focus on ease of living and ease of doing business. Economic reforms, no doubt, played a key role but understated has been the role of the new paradigm in governance. Citizens were now being delivered government benefits through digital means. Offline forms gave way to online single-window clearances. States were competing on who provided the easiest business environment.

The scale of reform has been truly exceptional. Having driven some flagship initiatives personally, such as ease of doing business and competition among states, Make in India, Startup India and production linked incentive (PLI) schemes, among others, I have seen how India's policy priorities have evolved during this time, and the same is reflected in 'A New Paradigm: Revitalizing the Economy'.

The importance of and trust in private enterprise now is worlds apart from the environment prevailing during the post-Independence period. There is an increasing acceptance among policymakers that engaging with private enterprise will usher in India's socio-economic transformation. This has perhaps been one of the biggest shifts in the attitudes of policymakers.

India's start-up ecosystem is now among the most vibrant in the world. Entrepreneurship is no longer looked down upon. The youth of today are now shunning the safety of jobs and instead following their dreams of entrepreneurship. New business models and novel solutions are being developed by these start-ups for some of India's legacy problems. Not just in e-commerce, entrepreneurs are innovating in health, agriculture and digital lending, among others. In addition to the evolution of India's private enterprise and the associated economic policies, this is also the story of the ingenuity, adaptability and risk-taking ability of our entrepreneurs. Budding entrepreneurs are certain to find inspiration in these stories.

It is this entrepreneurial zeal that we must rely on to tackle climate change, which is the world's biggest challenge to global prosperity and development. Policies to catalyse private action will hold the key in this battle. Over the past few years, India has emerged as a leader in the fight against climate change. Again, it has been a combination of public and private action. Enabling policies have seen private investments thrive in the renewable energy space. India's corporates are leading our green hydrogen charge. Start-ups are innovating in eMobility and the circular economy. Many leading corporates have taken the pledge to go net-zero by 2050. India's model of digital and green growth will make a telling contribution in ensuring the world's future.

This book also contributes to the understanding of India's economic history. Apart from informing readers of the evolution of India's private enterprise, it offers them a primer of the evolution of the economy and economic policies. The lessons we learn from the past will serve us well as we enter the next phase of our industrial journey. It is important to understand the context in which these policies evolved. Readers can expect to find an analysis of key policy decisions taken since the post-Independence era. The rationale and impact of these policies are evaluated against global best practices of the time. As our Asian peers galloped away, over time, it became clear that the model India was following was not working.

The centrality of growth—a key takeaway from the Asian growth stories—is another recurring theme in the book. While India launched several socio-economic development programmes, it was only when growth was unleashed did India make a serious dent in poverty. Through this book, readers will appreciate the fine balance policy has to strike between growth and redistribution. The importance of looking outwards has also been reiterated. However, to thrive on a global stage, India must be competitive enough to become an integral part of global value chains (GVCs). This is the essence behind Aatmanirbhar Bharat (Self-reliant India), which many have confused to mean looking inwards.

While the book discusses the growth stories of Asia and brings forth policy lessons, there are new challenges that India now faces. The environment in which India is seeking to integrate itself in GVCs is vastly different to when Japan, South Korea or China saw their transformations. While other advanced countries grew and prospered with carbon emissions, India has promised to cut its emissions to net zero by 2070. This is not only a challenge but also an opportunity. Digital technologies are permeating economies like never before. Global trade has been slowing. The economies that can turn these challenges into opportunities will be the most competitive in the future. In addition to reviewing and analysing the evolution of our economic policies, the book also takes a forward-looking view.

This book required knowledge of India's political economy, its socialist roots and turn towards private sector enterprise. The sharp command over these subjects displayed by Economist and Policy Specialist Ranveer Nagaich was an asset to the book. The book also benefitted from his exposure to India's policymaking through his stint at NITI Aayog and G20. India's private sector has undergone a sea change over the last few years and Ranveer was not only in the front seat but also, through his stint at NITI, contributed to this transformation. He is a brilliant young scholar with a natural appetite for data-driven insights, deep understanding of policy issues, lucid writing and relentless curiosity. The book benefitted immensely from his intellectual contribution.

Having spent six-and-a-half years at NITI Aayog and now as India's G20 Sherpa, I have always encouraged my colleagues to be futuristic in their thinking. It is technology and sunrise sectors of growth that will enable a new era of prosperity in India's growth story. This book highlights the new avenues of growth and competitiveness and lays out a strategy for what India must do to achieve its aspirations. I hope readers enjoy reading this book as much as I enjoyed writing it.

⌘

ONE

LEGACIES OF THE PAST

Trade and commerce have long been integral to India's history. This long history made us one of the dominant economic powers in the 1600s. Throughout these 400-odd years, the state of private enterprise and that of India's economy have been closely linked.[1]

As per the Maddison (2020) estimates,[2] India's share in the global gross domestic product (GDP) was 24 per cent in 1700. By 1820, this number fell to 16 per cent, and another 100-odd years later, in 1900, it dipped further to 8 per cent. By the time of Independence, this number had fallen to 5 per cent. So, in 250-odd years, India went from contributing a quarter of global GDP to less than 5 per cent. From being one of the largest economies in the pre-industrial revolution era, India shifted to the peripheries of global trade and commerce by the time of Independence.

The world, too, has seen considerable churn since then. The Industrial Revolution, advances in communication and innovations in transport, such as the railways and steamships, brought the world closer together. Yet, this was also a time of significant political upheaval. In Europe, empires were gradually making way for the modern nation states we see today. New countries were born out of colonies in North America, while new colonies were being created in Asia and Africa. Ideas of capitalism and communism appeared. The world wars unleashed a wave of destruction and loss not seen before.

With the Mughal Empire on its last legs, regional kingdoms in India flourished and were formidable in their own right. At the same

---

[1] Private enterprise is taken to have a wide-ranging definition in the book. It includes industry, trade, commerce and other service-based industries that have emerged.

[2] Maddison Project Database, version 2020. Bolt, Jutta, and Jan Luiten van Zanden, 'Maddison style estimates of the evolution of the world economy. A new 2020 update', 2020, https://bit.ly/3utZoHU, accessed on 6 July 2022.

time, European influence increased significantly. There are a few watershed moments we are all familiar with: the Battle of Plassey in 1757, which solidified the position of the East India Company (EIC), is one. The First War of Independence of 1857, which saw the British Raj begin, is another. This is no doubt less than even a cursory sketch of the great political, social, technological and economic upheaval the world saw between the 1700s to the time of India's independence. The outcome of this upheaval was that India lost its leading role in the global economy during this time. Colonialism was no doubt a major factor. New technologies in manufacturing, communication and transport drove competitiveness in European economies, while their colonies served as bases to acquire cheap raw material. Yet, the late colonial era saw the emergence of Indian industries and industrialists. Industry, trade and commerce, which drove India's dominance in the precolonial, Industrial Revolution era, was largely led by private enterprise. India's extensive trade network has been well-documented as well. The state, then defined as various monarchies, was rarely involved in trade and commerce beyond taxation.

Clearly, Indian enterprise has evolved from this complex history—a mix of socio-economic and political forces. This chapter traces some of the legacies of the past to better understand the evolution of the Indian private business class by the time of Independence. It attempts to understand the state of India's entrepreneurs and businesses in the precolonial, Industrial Revolution era and the subsequent impact of colonization. By the time colonial rule was solidified through the Government of India Act 1858 passed by the British parliament, India's position in the global economy had dwindled considerably. Yet, at the turn of the century, Indian business and enterprise started making a comeback and competing with their European counterparts. The chapter also discusses the evolution of these entrepreneurs and enterprises from the late colonial era to the time of Independence. It also attempts to understand the *Bombay Plan*, a memorandum put forward by Indian industrialists for the country's economic development on the eve of Independence, in 1944.

Emergence of Private Enterprise

D.R. Gadgil[3] and Dwijendra Tripathi[4] describe the state of India's private enterprise c.1700–50. India's long history and the predominance of the caste system imply that cultural and societal norms impacted the evolution of the country's private enterprise. Trading, banking and general business activities remained in the domain of a few castes, communities or regions. Gadgil notes that in urban India of the 1750s, the 'general trader-merchant class held a high socio-economic position'. Apart from taxes, there was little to no political interference, and despite holding a high socio-economic position, political influence was scant.

Family-run businesses dominated the landscape and remained in the realm of trade and commerce. Gadgil also notes that no formal forms of enterprise, such as joint-stock ventures, seemed to have been embraced, though individual family businesses persisted over generations and some were even able to accumulate significant resources. He also notes that these trader-merchants had little to no involvement in industry, and while the bankers provided loans, it was rarely risk capital. Investments by them were mostly limited to their homes or in jewellery.

Production of various goods (handicrafts, cloth, etc.) was carried out by artisans and craftsmen. Interestingly, there existed

---

[3]Gadgil, D.R., and M.V. Namjoshi, *Origins of the Modern Indian Business Class: An Interim Report*, Institute of Pacific Relations, New York, 1959.
[4]Tripathi, Dwijendra, *The Oxford History of Indian Business*, Oxford University Press India, 2004, Chapter 2.

trade guilds, which were a sort of informal, self-regulation mechanism. Trading rules were prescribed, and disputes settled by the elders of the guild. In South India, traders' associations existed since the fifteenth century. The most documented system comes from Gujarat, where craft guilds known as *mahajans,* headed by a *sheth,* functioned as early trade associations. In Surat, there is evidence of a general assembly of merchants, comprising various mahajans, headed by a *nagarsheth* (the chief merchant of the city). This can be thought of as an early precursor to the modern industry associations we see today.

Another feature discussed by Gadgil is the disaggregated nature of India's enterprises. This has been further corroborated by Tripathi. Slow modes of transport discouraged internal trade, and small, regional markets, rather than large, unified ones, developed in India. Security of trading caravans was an increasing issue as the Mughal Empire crumbled. Various currencies in circulation also hampered the development of markets. Tripathi estimates that close to a thousand currencies were in circulation during the nineteenth century in India.[5]

Consequently, the Indian economy of those days consisted of a vast number of decentralized, often unconnected markets. The size of the market depended on the commodity being traded. To overcome the connectivity problem, trader-merchants often employed brokers or middlemen, who procured commodities for them. This system evolved well in advance of European arrival. We can still see traces of this system, especially in India's agricultural markets.

Even though private enterprise in precolonial India consisted of trader-merchants, artisans, weavers, craftsmen, etc., some roots

[5]Tripathi, Dwijendra, 'Indian Entrepreneurship in Historical Perspective: A Re-Interpretation', *Economic & Political Weekly*, 6(22): M59–M66, 29 May 1971, https://bit.ly/3Pbuv37, accessed on 6 July 2022.

of specialization were taking place, especially in the domain of finance and broking. Gadgil notes that banking houses (or banks) specialized in three functions. Given the number of currencies in circulation in India, the first was money changing. Issuing bills of exchange was another important function performed with sophisticated security practices. The bigger banking houses usually had a pan-India reach through a network of correspondents. Government finance was the third important role they played.

India's Deindustrialization

The impact of colonial policy on Indian industry has been well-documented by several scholars. From being a net exporter of goods for much of its history, India became a net importer, especially in areas where we had an advantage, such as garments and textiles.

The 'deindustrialization' of India during this period has garnered significant debate.[6] There are two views, primarily. The first is that Indian manufacturing in textiles lost competitiveness. Bishnupriya Gupta notes that India's competitive advantage in the textile sector rested on the skills of the weavers, the quality of the raw material and low wages.[7] Yet, the sector saw no major technological change in the two centuries prior to the Industrial Revolution. The Industrial Revolution in Great Britain brought down the prices of textiles, and steam-powered vessels, canals, etc., drove down transportation costs. So, the deindustrialization

---

[6]Clingingsmith, David, and Jeffrey G. Williamson, 'Deindustrialization in 18th and 19th Century India: Mughal Decline, Climate Shocks and British Industrial Ascent', *Explorations in Economic History*, 45(3): 209–34, July 2008.

[7]Gupta, Bishnupriya, 'Falling Behind and Catching Up: India's Transition from a Colonial Economy', *The Economic History Review*, 72(3): 803–27, August 2019, https://bit.ly/3AhUMqw, accessed on 24 August 2022.

of India was an effect of eroding competitiveness. However, David Clingingsmith and Jeffrey G. Williamson argue that it was due to supply side issues, rather than global price movements that Indian industry lost competitiveness.[8] The political upheaval post the dissolution of the Mughal Empire, natural calamities and other factors have also been cited as issues of eroding competitiveness of Indian industry during this period.

As colonialism took root, there was a disruption in trading patterns and new forms of banking, managing agencies and chambers of commerce emerged during British rule, Jayati Bhattacharya notes.[9] Authors such as Tirthankar Roy[10] have argued that the colonial period created opportunities for private enterprise to thrive on, which many entrepreneurs capitalized. These views have also been echoed by Dwijendra Tripathi and Makrand Mehta,[11] who claim that the success of European entrepreneurs in India, through the use of technology and better management, spurred Indian entrepreneurship. Their argument rests on the premise that the success of Europeans raised the perception among Indian communities of the profitability of such enterprises.

The argument that the new ways of doing business encouraged Indians towards entrepreneurship rests on the same premise as the impact generated by the railways. Large-scale investments in the

---

[8]Clingingsmith, David, and Jeffrey G. Williamson, 'Deindustrialization in 18th and 19th Century India: Mughal Decline, Climate Shocks and British Industrial Ascent', *Explorations in Economic History*, 45(3): 209–34, July 2008.

[9]Bhattacharya, Jayati, 'The Story of Indian Business: The Great Transition into the New Millennium', Education about Asia: Online Archives, Association for Asian Studies, 24(2), Fall 2019.

[10]Roy, Tirthankar, *A Business History of India: Enterprise and the Emergence of Capitalism from 1700*, Cambridge University Press, Cambridge, 2018.

[11]Tripathi, Dwijendra, and Makrand Mehta, *Business Houses in Western India: A Study in Entrepreneurial Response, 1850-1956*, Manohar Publishers and Distributors, 1990.

railways by the British reduced trading costs, closed price gaps and increased trade flows within India. However, many others have emphatically argued that investments in railways were primarily intended to serve the interests of first the EIC and then Great Britain.[12] The business environment argument can be evaluated similarly. Mechanisms to enhance business efficiency were introduced to facilitate European businesses, traders and merchants.

On the other hand, a recurring critique of colonial rule has been that policies were introduced precisely to erode competitiveness. For instance, raw cotton was sent to Britain, duty-free, and processed in factories. The finished goods were then sent back to India, again duty-free. So, not only were India's export markets closed off, the domestic market, too, was subject to cheap imports. By 1880, British imports accounted for 60 per cent of domestic consumption, Gupta notes.[13]

Industry became less relevant in the colonial economy, and agricultural commodities became the predominant exports. Opium exports to China grew, which were used to pay for imports of tea by Britain. Gupta also notes that while capital did flow to India, it was mainly for the railroads, and no major investments were made to improve agricultural productivity. She states that 'the nationalists saw this as exploitation that cemented India's relationship with the Empire as a supplier of agricultural products and a market of British industrial goods'.[14]

Gupta has also provided evidence for paucity of investments in primary schooling by the colonial government. According to

---

[12]Tharoor, Shashi, *An Era of Darkness: The British Empire in India*, Aleph Book Company, 2016.

[13]Gupta, Bishnupriya, 'Falling Behind and Catching Up: India's Transition from a Colonial Economy', *The Economic History Review*, 72(3): 803–27, August 2019, https://bit.ly/3AhUMqw, accessed on 24 August 2022.

[14]Ibid. 14.

Latika Chaudhary and Manuj Garg, public investment in education by the colonial government was among the lowest in the world, and that India's princely states in fact invested more in education than the colonial government.[15] Whatever amount of public investment was made by the colonial government in education was primarily to serve imperial interests. Thus, a drain of financial resources, deindustrialization and a lack of public investments in agriculture and education meant that the colonial economy was repurposed to serve imperial needs. The Indian economy, once dominant in global trade, was moved to the fringes.

Resurgence in Industry

At the formal start of the British Raj, while Indian industry suffered considerably, trade and commerce, in all likelihood, suffered as well from the falling industrial output. However, within a few decades, a resurgence in Indian industry has been identified. The trader-merchants identified by Gadgil were now moving to industry. As laws and rules were formalized, the 'industrial capitalist' class in India emerged from a 'process of merchants turning producers', argues Surajit Mazumdar.[16]

Indian enterprise then began to adapt to the changing times. Gadgil had noted that around the 1750s, Indian enterprises retained a non-corporate character. Over the next hundred years, Mazumdar finds that a distinct corporate character in Indian enterprises emerged, as extensive use was made of the joint-stock companies. The Joint-Stock Companies Act of 1857 facilitated the creation of a corporate sector.

---

[15]Chaudhary, Latika, and Manuj Garg, 'Does History Matter? Colonial Education Investments in India', *The Economic History Review*, 68(3): 937–61, August 2015.
[16]Mazumdar, Surajit, *The Incomplete Transition: Stunted Industrialisation and the Historical Development of India's Big Business Class*, Munich Personal RePEc Archive, 30 December 2018, https://bit.ly/3pHoSPo, accessed on 24 August 2022.

One of the defining features of this era is the proliferation and dominance of managing agencies in the corporate sector, which is unique to the history of colonial India. The idea was simple: a managing agent (which could be an individual or a company) would be hired to manage joint-stock companies. The control offered to such agents was wide-ranging—from carrying out all management-related functions to raising finance, with very small portions of actual shares in the companies they managed.[17] The genesis of such a system can be traced to the time of the EIC, where agency houses facilitated transfer of money of EIC officials between India and Britain. Gradually, these agencies became involved in trade and commerce and eventually took on the role of managers of these joint-stock companies. At first glance, this system, in theory, seems no different from the separation of management and ownership prevalent in management literature.

Over the years, these firms built reserves of capital and developed expertise in domestic and international markets, making them professional managers of that era. The popularity of the managing agency system was also driven by Indian social realities. The family management system was formalized through the managing agency system, allowing the family to retain control over core businesses and assets. While the managing agency system saw considerable opposition and eventually its abolishment by the Government of India (GoI) in 1970, it nonetheless played an important role in the development of modern Indian enterprise.

In the late 1800s, Indian entrepreneurs and enterprises began to make their mark both domestically and internationally. Cotton was an early success story of Indian industry. Factories set up

---

[17]Varottil, Umakanth, 'The Evolution of Corporate Law in Post-Colonial India: From Transplant to Autochthony', *American University International Law Review*, Vol. 31, pp. 253–325, 2016.

in the Bombay-Ahmedabad region using imported machinery became more competitive than British industry and soon gained domestic market share.

Cowaszee Nanabhoy Davar, who established the Bombay Spinning and Weaving Company in Bombay in 1854, can be considered a pioneer. Jamsetji Tata established Alexandra Mill in 1869, selling it for a profit, before establishing the Central India Spinning, Weaving and Manufacturing Company in 1874. Within three years, Empress Mills commenced operations. Bombay Dyeing was established by the Wadia Group in 1879. In Ahmedabad, Calico Mills came up in 1880 under the tutelage of the Sarabhai family. DCM Textiles was founded by Lala Sri Ram in 1889 in Delhi.

The other main 'modern' industries, as described by Gupta, were tea and jute, which were financed and dominated by British businesses.[18]

Soon, Indian companies were making forays into industries apart from cotton. This is perhaps best exemplified by the wide-ranging vision and nationalistic fervour of Jamsetji Tata. His vision included an iron and steel company, hydroelectric power, a world-class educational institute and a world-class hotel catering to Indians (i.e. the Tata Group). The iconic Taj Mahal Hotel came to life in 1903. The Tata Iron and Steel Company, later renamed Tata Steel, was founded by Jamsetji in 1907 and completed by Sir Dorabji Tata. Tata Power was born in 1910, making it India's first hydroelectric plant. In 1909, the Indian Institute of Science was established in Bangalore owing to the joint efforts of Jamsetji Tata, the GoI and the Maharaja of Mysore. The year 1912 saw India's first planned industrial city, Jamshedpur, established.

---

[18]Gupta, Bishnupriya, 'Falling Behind and Catching Up: India's Transition from a Colonial Economy', *The Economic History Review*, 72(3): 803–27, August 2019, https://bit.ly/3AhUMqw, accessed on 24 August 2022.

Kirloskar Brothers Limited, established in 1888, was among the first to venture into engineering industries in India. Around the same time, the Birla family was making their fortunes in trading of cotton and opium. When Ghanshyam Das Birla entered the family business, he steered it in the direction of manufacturing. The monopoly of the British in jute manufacturing was overcome by him when he became one of the first Indians to own a jute mill, eventually diversifying into sectors such as aluminium, cement, automobiles and chemicals.

In construction, Shapoorji Pallonji was established in 1865 and has built numerous historical landmarks in Mumbai. Ardeshir Godrej established the Godrej Group in 1897 with the manufacturing of locks. In 1918, the group launched the world's first vegetable oil-based soap. In 1923, they ventured into furniture, and Godrej almirahs became a permanent fixture in Indian households. Few people know that Godrej manufactured the ballot boxes for India's first general election in 1951. The twentieth century also saw the advent of the Walchand Group, founded by Walchand Hirachand Doshi. The Singhania family rose to prominence in Kanpur and the J.K. Organisation was established in 1918. Today, through various headquarters in Kanpur, Delhi and Mumbai, companies such as JK Cement, JK Tyre and Raymond are run. The Murugappa Group was founded in 1900. The TVS Group sees its roots stretch back to 1911, established by T.V. Sundaram Iyengar. The Bajaj Group was established in 1926. Bajaj would go on to play a pivotal role in developing India's two- and three-wheeler manufacturing industry. They began manufacturing in 1959, and introduced the famous Chetak model in 1972. In 1977, they launched the rear engine autorickshaw, ubiquitous with India's urban transport landscape. Their memorable 'Hamara Bajaj' campaign touched many hearts when it was launched.

The Chemical, Industrial and Pharmaceutical Laboratories (Cipla) was founded by Khwaja Abdul Hamied in 1935. Wipro, too, traces its history back to the pre-Independence era. The Mahindra group was founded in 1945, starting with steel trading. A few years later, the Willys Jeep was introduced in India and it quickly became a favourite, establishing itself firmly as part of the country's fabric, along with Hindustan Motors's Ambassador. The Mahindra Brothers were one of the first to leverage foreign expertise to build domestic capabilities.

Banking is another area where Indians and Indian enterprise thrived. The Punjab National Bank was founded in 1894 as the first bank with Indian capital. Lala Lajpat Rai was involved in the management of the bank in its early years. The Bank of India was founded in Bombay in 1906 by a group of industrialists including Ratanji Tata. Sayajirao Gaekwad III, along with other industrialists, set up the Bank of Baroda in 1908. The Central Bank of India was founded in 1911 and the Indian Overseas Bank in 1937. Many other banks were created in the pre-Independence era, and it was private enterprise that took the lead in establishing a modern banking sector in India. Many of these banks were nationalized later and continue to be some of the largest banks in India.

Many of the names discussed above and several others not mentioned here had a leading role to play in the Indian independence movement, in building a national identity and in investing in human capital. In fact, many of these industrialists are seen as some of the greatest philanthropists of their times as well.

Clearly, Indian entrepreneurs had rekindled India's industrialization efforts, despite functioning in a colonial economy. However, the fact remained and recognized by many of the industrialists that India's industrial base was narrow and needed to be widened. Industrialization at a wide scale was still needed. In terms of regional distribution, Indian enterprises, meant as those owned and financed by Indians, were mostly concentrated in the Mumbai-Ahmedabad region of today. In Bengal, for instance, jute manufacturing was solely in the hands of British firms, and in Kanpur, all of the mills were British owned and financed.

Created by Business, for Business

Even as industry and private enterprise were expanding in India, a lack of investments in agriculture and education meant that income gaps with the rest of the world expanded during this time. Cognizant of these gaps, and the need to broad-base industrial growth in India, a group of leading industrialists comprising J.R.D Tata, Ghanshyam Das Birla, Sir Purshotamdas Thakurdas, Sir Shri Ram and John Mathai, among others, banded together to imagine what independent India's economy would look like. They published *A Plan of Economic Development for India*, commonly known as the *Bombay Plan*, in 1944.[19]

A little earlier, as Independence approached, the Congress appointed the National Planning Committee (NPC) in 1938, to design economic policies for an independent India. Central planning and the public sector at the 'commanding heights' are some ideas from those times.[20]

The two plans agreed on the need for rapid industrialization and central planning. However, there were some crucial differences. While both approaches involved central planning

[19]Baru, Sanjaya, and Meghnad Desai (eds), *The Bombay Plan: Blueprint for Economic Resurgence*, Rupa Publications, New Delhi, 2018.
[20]Guha, Ramachandra, *India After Gandhi: The History of the World's Largest Democracy*, Macmillan/Picador, London, 2007; Engerman, David C., *The Price of Aid: The Economic Cold War in India*, Harvard University Press: Illustrated edition, 2018.

and an important role accorded to the public sector, the *Bombay Plan* differed in some areas. First, it saw an expanded role for India in global trade. Second, it saw government support for development of private industry, rather than control. Furthermore, the size and the role of the public sector were up for debate as well. While the NPC saw public-sector enterprises (PSEs) as the drivers of industrialization and transformation, the *Bombay Plan* saw a supporting role for the public sector, investing in areas where private capital was lacking. Energy, infrastructure and transport were areas where government monopolies were advised by the *Bombay Plan*.

The *Bombay Plan* envisaged a doubling of India's per capita income within 15 years. The Plan also called for creating industries for the production of power and capital goods. Industry was divided into two segments: basic goods and consumer goods. Basic industries included power, mining and metallurgy, engineering, chemicals, transport, armaments and cement. These industries were seen as the foundation of India's industrial transformation by the authors of the Plan. The Plan noted that consumer goods manufacturing, at the same time, should not be neglected. Small-scale industries were given a prominent role in the manufacturing of consumer goods, recognizing that the scope for small industries in basic goods industries was limited owing to the scale.

In terms of the structure of the economy, it targeted a doubling of the share in industry from 17 per cent to 35 per cent, compensated for by declining shares in agriculture. Raising irrigation coverage, ensuring soil health and increasing productivity were some of the issues touched upon in agriculture. Increasing the average size of the farm, preferably through cooperative farming, to intensify agriculture, was one of their key proposals as well. Furthermore, the sole focus of the Plan was not on industrial and commercial development either. They defined the standard of living as including not just income but also a balanced diet, shelter, clothing, health and education. Public health was divided into preventive measures, including sanitation, water supply, vaccination, anti-epidemic procedures and curative measures, which included medical facilities.

What is interesting is the economic system on which the *Bombay Plan* rested. At the outset, the authors recognized an important role for a central planning authority in determining the feasibility of the Plan. However, they also emphasized that it was entirely possible to have economic planning in a democratic society, and the Soviet style of planning was not the only model to follow. A strong role for the private sector was envisioned, both in basic and consumer industries. Giving due to each school of thought, the authors elucidated three principles underlying their choice of economic system, stating,

> First, that there should be sufficient scope for the play of individual initiative and enterprise; secondly that the interests of the community should be safeguarded by the institution of adequate sanctions against the abuse of individual freedom, and thirdly, that the State should play a positive role in the direction of economic policy and the development of economic resources.[21]

The proposed *Bombay Plan* soon dominated discussions surrounding India's economic future. This is perhaps an early example of private sector-led efforts to design an economic road map for India. Many of the ideas of the *Bombay Plan* overlapped with the NPC of the Congress. However, the crucial difference remained in the role of the public and private sectors.

---

[21]Baru, Sanjaya, and Meghnad Desai (eds), *The Bombay Plan: Blueprint for Economic Resurgence*, Rupa Publications, New Delhi, 2018.

Government ownership of industry was seen as crucial by the Congress Working Committee. It leaves us to wonder that if the *Bombay Plan* had panned out, India's economic trajectory could have been much different.

❦

TWO

FROM BRITISH RAJ
TO LICENCE RAJ

lanning occupied a central role in India's economic policies in the post-Independence era. Even the *Bombay Plan* put forward by industrialists called for a large role for the public sector and centralized planning to achieve India's goals. The Plan saw the government supporting the private sector in industrializing India.

However, much of the political leadership saw it differently. Initially, the mixed-economy model was envisioned for India, where both the public and the private sector would have roles to play in the economy. Import substitution was the approach taken to develop domestic industry. Barriers to trade were erected to protect domestic industry from foreign competition. The production of capital goods over consumer goods was emphasized. A leading role for the public sector in developing industry was seen. Jayati Bhattacharya states that there was a growing antipathy towards capitalism, as it was synonymized with colonialism.[1] Rather than developing private industry, the state would play the role of the entrepreneur, as reinforced by the industrialization of the Soviet Union through the Five-Year Plans (FYPs).

Thus began a new political and economic climate for Indian business and enterprise. Industrial policies placing the state at the 'commanding heights of the economy', centralized planning and a complex system of licences and regulations dominated India's economic spheres in the years following Independence. This position of the state at the commanding heights was consolidated when Indira Gandhi was elected as prime minister (PM) in 1966. Banking, insurance and coal mining saw nationalization. High levels of marginal taxation saw a narrow tax base develop. Thus, India's economic policies in the post-Independence era took us

[1] Bhattacharya, Jayati, 'The Story of Indian Business: The Great Transition into the New Millennium', Education about Asia: Online Archives, Association for Asian Studies, 24(2), Fall 2019.

from the British Raj to the Licence Raj, with a debilitating impact on business and enterprise.

Centralized Planning Landscape

The need for centralized planning was agreed upon by the private sector and the government alike as reiterated by the NPC of the Congress in 1938 and the *Bombay Plan* in 1944, which had elucidated the need for a central planning body to direct resources and investments. No doubt, the transformation of the Soviet Union from an agrarian economy to an industrial powerhouse had an influence.

In 1946, the Advisory Planning Board appointed by the interim government recommended the creation of an organization for planning. Interestingly, this body was recommended to be advisory in nature, apolitical and to draw on experience of experts through various committees. The Economic Programme Committee of the All India Congress Committee made a similar recommendation in 1948. In 1950, through a Cabinet Resolution, the Planning Commission came into being. The chairman would be the PM, and a deputy-chairman and members would form the rest of the Planning Commission, supported by a secretariat. It was to be an advisory body but gradually evolved into a powerful institution. Twelve FYPs have since been introduced, as Table 1 illustrates.

Table 1: India's Five-Year Plans

Five-Year Plan	Time Period
First FYP	1951–56
Second FYP	1956–61
Third FYP	1961–66
Annual Plan	1966–69

Fourth FYP	1969–74
Fifth FYP	1974–79
Annual Plan	1979–80
Sixth FYP	1980–85
Seventh FYP	1985–90
Annual Plan	1990–92
Eighth FYP	1992–97
Ninth FYP	1997–2002
Tenth FYP	2002–07
Eleventh FYP	2007–12
Twelfth FYP	2012–17

By most accounts, the First Plan was a success. Against a targeted growth rate of 2.6 per cent, a rate of 3.5–4 per cent was achieved, depending on which base we are using to measure the gross domestic product (GDP). The focus was on irrigation, power and community development projects to deal with the aftermath of Partition. While industrialization through heavy industry was high on the policy agenda, the First Plan dealt with the immediate challenges that arose following Partition.

From the Second Plan onwards, we see an expanded role for the public sector. Here, in the objectives, the phrase 'socialistic pattern of society' was used. In the words of the Planning Commission, this meant:

> [...] the basic criterion for determining the lines of advance must not be private profit, but social gain and that the pattern of development and the structure of socio-economic relations should be so planned that they result not only in appreciable increases in national income and employment, but also in greater equality in incomes and wealth. Major decisions regarding production, distribution, consumption

and investment [...] must be made by agencies informed
by social purpose.[2]

The development of the plan was led by P.C. Mahalanobis, and
the approach paper elucidated the need for the leading role
to be taken by the public sector. The rationale being that the
adoption of modern technology to develop industry necessitated
state intervention in order to direct investments towards where
it was most needed. Minerals and basic capital goods industries
were seen as the major determinants of growth by the Plan,
and therefore these needed to be in public control. It was
admitted that in the rest of the economy, conditions for the
private sector to grow had to be created. However, the Industrial
Policy Resolution of 1956 saw a role for the private sector mostly
in the consumer goods industry, and not in capital goods, as
envisioned by the *Bombay Plan*.

Within the first year of the Second Plan, India was plunged
into a foreign exchange (forex) crisis. While the total outflow of
forex reserves during the First Plan amounted to ₹158 crore, within
a little less than 15 months of the Second Plan, it amounted to
₹278 crore.[3] It is this surge in imports that led to the exchange
rate crisis. Economist B.R. Shenoy blamed deficit spending for
the creation of excess demand in the economy, which spilled over
into the external sector as well as created inflation.

The crisis years of 1956–58 saw voices raised in favour of
increased private-sector participation in capital goods, export
orientation and foreign investment, as David C. Engerman

---

[2] Planning Commission, *Second Five-Year Plan, Approach to the Second Five-Year Plan*, Government of India, New Delhi, 1957, p. 22, https://bit.ly/3R7W3ap, accessed on 25 August 2022.

[3] Rao, VKRV, 'The Foreign Exchange Crisis and India's Second Five Year Plan', *Economic & Political Weekly*, 9(26-28), 6 July 1957.

details in his fascinating account.[4] A notable proponent was T.T. Krishnamachari, known as T.T.K., who was first the minister of commerce and industry at the time and later the minister of finance. An industrialist, he founded the TTK Group in 1928, which today is a conglomerate. However, as Gurcharan Das notes in *India Unbound*, T.T.K., as minister of industry, had authored the Industrial Policy Resolution of 1956, which significantly expanded state control and influence over industry.[5]

During this time, we also heard perhaps the first calls for a coherent foreign direct investment (FDI) policy. Among these people was Ghanshyam Das Birla, urging a more liberal climate for foreign investment. He not only called for policies to allow investments but also to allow Indians to retain control of their industries. However, these voices were in the minority. Imports of consumer goods raised the import bill. Draining reserves was the contention of the Planning Commission. Greater control over consumption and imports would be required to save forex. Even PM Jawaharlal Nehru acknowledged that the Second Plan, while ambitious, gave little space to the financing of the actual plan.[6] External aid became a dominant source of funding, with the Third Plan envisioning an important role for it, which was absent from the first two plans. Strict capital controls were put in place, and allocation of reserves became the key objective of trade and forex policy. Consistent with the political climate of the time, foreign trade and investment were perhaps viewed with even more suspicion than domestic private enterprise.

[4]Engerman, David C., *The Price of Aid: The Economic Cold War in India*, Harvard University Press, 2018.
[5]Das, Gurcharan, *India Unbound: From Independence to Global Information Age*, Penguin Books India, New Delhi, 2015.
[6]Engerman, David C., *The Price of Aid: The Economic Cold War in India*, Harvard University Press, 2018.

However, as Arvind Panagariya notes, elements of trade liberalization and control were seen during the First Plan, with tariffs being raised but import quotas liberalized, through an Open General Licence (OGL) list.[7] However, the forex crisis of 1956–57 prompted a firm reversal. Managing forex came to the top of the agenda. A complex, protectionist trade regime was put firmly in place.

While the FYPs outlined the goals, objectives and financial resources available, administrative mechanisms needed to be created to implement these plans. This was achieved through Industrial Policy, most notably the Industrial Policy Resolution of 1956. The genesis of this lies with the Industrial Policy Resolution of 1948, in which the leading role of the state in industrial development was outlined. Arms and ammunition, atomic energy and railways would be monopolies of the central government. State governments would further control six basic industries, which included coal, iron and steel, aircraft manufacture, shipbuilding and communications equipment (telephones, telegraphs, etc.). Industries ranging from salt and automobiles to cement, sugar and paper, among others, were open to the private sector. However, these would be planned and regulated by the central government and would remain open to public-sector participation as well.

The Industries (Development and Regulation) Act, 1951, provided the legislative framework. It is through this Act that the extensive permits and licencing system was created. Licences for starting new industries as well as for expanding and manufacturing new products were introduced. Right at the outset, major capital goods-producing industries were kept in the ambit of either the central or the state government, with the private sector operating

---

[7]Panagariya, Arvind, 'India's Trade Reform', *India Policy Forum*, Vol. 1, Brookings Institution Press, 2004.

in the consumer goods sector, under a strict regime of licences and permits.

This regime expanded further with the Industrial Policy Resolution of 1956, which created three categories under which industries were classified. The first category was reserved exclusively for the state, which would also take the lead in developing the second category, but there was some room for private-sector involvement too. The third category was the domain of the private sector, but the public sector reserved the right to enter these industries as well. With the systems in place, the government was now in a position to control where industries were located, how much they would produce and at what price. With legislation and relevant rules in place, the Licence Raj came into being. The greatest contribution of this legislation was the curbing of private enterprise.[8]

The goal of achieving a socialistic pattern of society meant that protecting the rights of labour were high on the agenda. The Industrial Disputes Act, 1947, was the first major legislation. Under this law, industrial firms looking to lay off workers needed government permission. The Factories Act, 1948, regulated worker safety and created an extensive system of inspections and criminal penalties. The Minimum Wages Act, 1948, established minimum wages. Since labour falls under the concurrent list of the Constitution, states enacted similar legislations. Labour law in trade and services was regulated through various state-level Shops and Establishments Acts. Social security systems were created through the Employees' State Insurance Act, 1948, and the Employees' Provident Funds and Miscellaneous Provisions Act, 1952. These are but a few labour laws that proliferated in India.

---

[8]Chikermane, Gautam, *70 Policies that Shaped India: 1947 to 2017, Independence to $2.5 Trillion*, Observer Research Foundation (ORF), 2018.

Doubling Down on Control: Nationalization

In the years following the Industrial Policy Resolution of 1956 and the Second Plan, instability perhaps best characterized the Indian economy. The India–China War of 1962 and the India–Pakistan War of 1965 reprioritized public expenditure towards national defence. Political instability at the highest level was also seen. The death of Nehru in 1964 brought in Lal Bahadur Shastri as PM, who reoriented public expenditure towards agriculture to raise production following a spate of droughts. In his short reign, Shastri led the country through war and rallied the nation to collectively combat food shortages. It was during this time that the Food Corporation of India was set up to procure food grains from farmers at minimum support prices announced through the Agriculture Prices Commission (precursor of today's Commission for Agricultural Costs & Prices). The incentives offered to farmers were hugely important in increasing production. Combined with Green Revolution policies, these measures helped improve productivity massively. The seeds of India's self-sufficiency in food production were sown during this time.

Shastri was succeeded by Mrs Gandhi as PM following his death in 1966. Inflation, food shortages and unemployment meant that the economy essentially teetered from one crisis to another. Shortages of forex were a constant highlight of this period. Apart from imports of capital and consumer goods, food imports, too, were rising to meet internal demand. This perhaps would have been an apt time to introduce outward-looking reforms, such as FDI and an export orientation, as many other Asian countries were pursuing. While there were some calls for reforms, the voices were not loud enough. Eventually, following the crisis of 1966, the rupee had to be devalued from ₹4.5/$ to ₹7.5/$ in Mrs Gandhi's first year as PM, accompanied by some liberalization of the trade regime. However, this coincided with a year of crop failure that plunged the economy into a recession. The response, predictably, was to further control imports and forex outflows.

This period also witnessed a spate of nationalizations. The first wave of nationalization was seen in the civil aviation sector, under the Air Corporations Act, 1953, where nine airlines were nationalized, including Air India. While J.R.D. Tata was appointed chairman of Indian Airlines and Air India, he found that government control stifled the running of the operations.[9] Life Insurance was nationalized in 1956, forming the Life Insurance Corporation of India.

Even though the development of the Indian banking industry was largely a private-sector driven exercise, during the period 1951–67, a consolidation in India's banking space took place, resulting in the number of commercial banks coming down from 566 in 1951 to 91 in 1967.[10] The Imperial Bank of India was nationalized in 1955 and renamed the State Bank of India. Post this consolidation, the health of the banking system improved and its reach expanded, albeit in urban areas. Rural India was still deprived of banking services. Credit was mainly being directed towards large industries, depriving agriculture and small-scale industries of credit. The criticisms were not entirely unfounded. The share of agriculture in credit remained stagnant at 2 per cent between 1951 and 1967, while the share of industry increased from 34 per cent in 1951 to 64.3 per cent in 1967.[11] Banks were not serving the social purpose, it was claimed.

[9]Ibid.

[10]Reserve Bank of India, *History of the Reserve Bank of India (1951–67): Volume II*, 2006.

[11]Agrawal, Amol, 'Why Indira Gandhi Nationalised India's Banks', *Bloomberg Quint*, 12 July 2019, https://bit.ly/3b0wloR, accessed on 21 July 2022.

Despite attempts at gaining more social control of banks in the months preceding nationalization, Mrs Gandhi decided to go ahead with nationalization of banks through the Banking Companies (Acquisition and Transfer of Undertakings) Act, 1970, which came into force in July 1969. Fourteen banks accounting for approx. 80 per cent of deposits were nationalized. This remains the defining event in India's economic history.

This trend of nationalization of industries continued. Coal was nationalized in 1971 followed by general insurance in 1972. Floundering textile units were nationalized under the Sick Textile Undertakings (Nationalization) Act, 1974. Further eight banks were nationalized in 1980.

It was not just private enterprise that was viewed with suspicion, as reflected through the policies enacted in the first 25 years of Independence. Foreign capital, too, was viewed with suspicion. With the enactment of the Foreign Exchange Regulation Act, 1973, foreign companies were asked to dilute their holdings to 40 per cent and had to apply for a licence to hold higher stakes. According to Chikermane, 881 companies applied, of which only 150 were granted licences.[12] By 1978, many companies chose to exit India, including IBM and Coca-Cola. Some foreign companies, such as Hindustan Unilever and Imperial Tobacco Company (later renamed Indian Tobacco Company or ITC), chose to comply and divested their equity.

An Inefficient, Uninventive and Rent-Seeking Economy

The policy framework introduced by the Industrial Policy Resolution of 1956 continued to govern India's industrial sector

---

[12]Chikermane, Gautam, *70 Policies that Shaped India: 1947 to 2017, Independence to $2.5 Trillion*, Observer Research Foundation (ORF), 2018, Chapter 26.

and was increasingly identified with an inefficient and uninventive economy. The government taking the leading role in investment in a resource-constrained environment meant that underinvestment remained a constant feature of the economy as the experience with the Second FYP shows. Forex shortages and subsequent crises were frequent. These forex crises emerged primarily due to surging imports, both of capital goods and consumer goods. With the government investing in heavy industry, investments in human capital and infrastructure suffered. These investments, while crucial initially, became inefficient and were not competitive globally. Being protected from both domestic and foreign competition meant that there were no incentives to innovate, become more efficient and lean in operations to drive productivity and competitiveness. This was true as much for the public sector as it was for the private sector. Competition brings innovation, and by choking off competition through protectionism, India fell further behind the industrial technological curve. Consumers were faced with poor-quality products and a lack of choices. 'Imported' goods got the connotation of being of a superior quality.

In 1967, certain products were made exclusive to small-scale industries, and they were also offered incentives. This again had the unintended impact of keeping industries and operations small. If the small-scale industries exceeded some thresholds of investment and output, they would lose the associated incentives and not be allowed to produce the products they had specialized in. Economies of scale were absent from India's economic landscape.

Inefficiency and a lack of expertise in implementing this extensive system of controls further strangled private enterprise. As Rakesh Mohan notes, a myriad of licences and permissions were needed at every step.[13] To start an enterprise, an entrepreneur first needed

---

[13]Mohan, Rakesh, 'The Road to the 1991 Industrial Policy Reforms and Beyond: A Personalized Narrative from the Trenches', *India Transformed: 25 Years of*

to get an 'in-principle' approval from the Ministry of Industry. This was followed by a 'letter of intent' (LoI), which contained a phased plan towards indigenization of manufacturing. This LoI was crucial in further steps. If imported capital goods were required, then an import licence was needed from the Chief Controller of Imports and Exports, under the Ministry of Commerce.

Licences, however, were granted through a committee headed by the Ministry of Industry. Separate import licences were required, renewable on an annual basis, for other raw materials and intermediate goods. Licences would take months to be granted, often based on the recommendations of bureaucrats and engineers with little experience of private enterprise. The need to get multiple licences meant that it could be a year before all the approvals were in place. For example, a factory looking to expand operations would need to get industrial licences and import licences, among others.

The Directorate General of Technical Development (DGTD) was the nodal agency to determine goods for which imports would be banned. It would often be that a domestic producer could approach the DGTD to seek a ban on an imported product. The DGTD was tasked with determining whether the producer possessed the technical capability to produce the goods in India. This hampered the import of capital and intermediate goods, thus hindering our industrial productivity and efficiency. Further permissions were needed from the Ministry of Finance if a foreign partner was involved, and if dipping into capital markets, permission from the Controller of Capital Issues. With a lack of clear direction and priorities, decisions were often made on an ad hoc basis. Foreign investment was subject to further review.

Just as the Second Plan essentially ignored financial constraints,

---

Economic Reforms, Rakesh Mohan (ed.), Penguin Random House India, New Delhi, 2017.

the industrial policy gave little thought to implementing the system of licencing and control. This also gave rise to opportunities for rent-seeking, commonly known as corruption. With an intricate web of controls in place, bribes and favours exploded. The system created incentives for both officers and entrepreneurs to surreptitiously encourage such behaviour. Expediting the granting of permits, licences and permissions are some examples. This system permeated throughout.

Strangling private enterprise was achieved not just through controls but also through various other laws, including labour laws. For instance, under the Industrial Disputes Act, 1947, the firing of employees of industrial establishments with a size of over 50 was subject to government approval. This discouraged scale in industry and formality in employment. Enterprises were reluctant to hire additional permanent employees, fearing that they would not be able to scale back operations when they needed to. Second, it encouraged enterprises to limit permanent employees to the thresholds, so as to fall outside the ambit of the Act. Resultantly, enterprises relied extensively on contract or informal labour, who were kept outside of the formal system of employment. They received no benefits, such as paid leave and insurance, among others, envisioned under these various laws, nor were they entitled to any of the social security measures proposed under the employees' provident fund and Employees' State Insurance Acts. So, rather than promoting formal, organized employment, the system of industrial controls and licencing promoted the informal and unorganized sector, where labour rights were rarely enforced.

Not only that, some of the provisions within these laws contained penal provisions. In fact, according to Gautam Chikermane and Rishi Agrawal, labour laws contained the most penal provisions. For instance, an entrepreneur could be sent to jail for failing to whitewash the walls of a factory or setting up spittoons or constituting a canteen committee. The threat of penal provisions further choked and discouraged private enterprise. As CEO, NITI Aayog, I chaired a number of meetings on decriminalization of such provisions and I hope the work continues with the same enthusiasm.[14]

Even after 75 years of Independence, we still find a large chunk of our labour force employed in the informal sector. Of course, a large chunk of this is in agriculture, but even if we take away the agriculture labour force, informal employment is still dominant in most sectors, including manufacturing and construction. This kept the economy in a low-productivity, low-wage and low-innovation loop, which persisted for decades.

Land, power and infrastructure emerged as other constraints owing to underinvestment, over-regulation and inefficient operations in PSEs. With PSEs at the commanding heights of the economy lacking any true competition, inefficiency and low productivity crept in. There were several reasons for this. First, the lack of competition meant that investments in research and development (R&D) and innovation were rarely high on the priority of the PSEs. The dynamism of private enterprise was also missing on the management side. Competition would have enabled greater focus on efficiency and productivity to compete in markets. Public resources were increasingly directed towards inefficient investments.

With the prevailing system, India's energies in entrepreneurship and innovation were not harnessed. Entrepreneurship was pretty much discouraged, with the youth of the day nudged towards 'safe' jobs in the government or as professionals such as doctors

[14]Chikermane, Gautam, and Rishi Agrawal, 'Jailed for Doing Business: The 26,134 Imprisonment Clauses in India's Business Laws', Observer Research Foundation, February 2022, https://bit.ly/3VTMHBn, accessed on 2 January 2023.

or engineers. Again, this nudge of 'safe' jobs excluded a large part of the population, as they lacked not just tertiary education to be successful in such jobs but also primary education. So, while a class of professionals emerged in India, it remained a small proportion, just like private enterprise.

Most younger readers today might not be able to fully appreciate the shortages and lack of choices faced by the youth of those times. My contemporaries would be more appreciable of the vast difference now. In fact, when I joined the Indian Administrative Service (IAS) in 1980, there were very few career opportunities. Since our family came from a government background, for me, therefore, the IAS was a logical course. However, I had never anticipated being appointed to the Kerala cadre. I was almost on the verge of quitting. But I ended up having the most wonderful experience in Kerala, starting with a posting as subcollector in Thalassery to being a collector in Calicut to driving the 'God's Own Country' campaign.

Back in those days, not just entrepreneurship, wealth creation, too, in general was discouraged—socially as well as through policy. Income and corporate tax rates were at levels one would find mind-boggling today. For example, in the early 1970s, the peak marginal income tax rate was at 97.5 per cent![15]

However, despite being shackled, private enterprises still navigated their way to growth. Grasim Industries was incorporated in 1947 and Hindalco in 1958. Hindustan Motors started manufacturing the Ambassador in 1957, while Premier Motors started manufacturing the Premier Padmini in 1964.

J.R.D. Tata expanded the Tata Empire during these times as well. Notably, Tata Consultancy Services (TCS) was founded in

[15]Govinda Rao, M., and R. Kavita Rao, 'Trends and Issues in Tax Policy and Reform in India', National Institute of Public Finance and Policy, India Policy Forum, 2006, https://brook.gs/3y0yh9R, accessed on 17 June 2022.

1968 as a division of Tata Sons. Lakmé, India's first homegrown cosmetics brand, was introduced by Tata Group and then later sold to Hindustan Unilever. Aditya Birla led an overseas expansion of the Group's interests, establishing their first overseas company in 1969. A visionary, Birla was ahead of his time in putting Indian businesses on the global map. Throughout his career, he set up 19 companies abroad. Frustrated with the Licence Raj and web of controls, he chose to expand abroad, rather than in India.[16] Perhaps the best example of building a conglomerate during these times is that of Dhirubhai Ambani, the founder of Reliance Industries. Starting in the fabrics and textiles industry, he soon oversaw a diversification to petrochemicals. Today, Reliance is one of India's largest conglomerates. O.P. Jindal established a steel plant in Haryana in 1952. Bharat Forge was established in 1961.

A Tale of Missed Opportunities

At a time where Asian countries were moving towards export promotion after protecting domestic private industry, India continued with inward-looking import substitution policies. Hence, economic growth, as confirmed by data, failed to reach the heights seen by other East Asian economies. Between 1950–51 and 1969–70, the economy grew at an average rate of 4 per cent in real terms, followed by 2.9 per cent in the next decade.[17] This supposed slow growth rate was termed the 'Hindu rate of growth', coined by economist Raj Krishna of the

---

[16]Birla, K., 'Butter Chicken at Birla', *Reimagining India: Unlocking the Potential of Asia's Next Superpower,* McKinsey & Company (eds), Simon & Schuster (first edition), 2013.

[17]Back series of National Accounts, 2011–12 base. Growth rates cited in this book throughout are based on the 2011–12 series, and as such, the growth rates mentioned here may differ from earlier estimates. The series begins in the year 1950–51 and is available on an annual basis till 2021.

Delhi School of Economics. Perhaps more importantly, in the same period, per capita income grew at less than half the rate of GDP (<2 per cent).

The share of manufacturing in GDP went from 9 per cent to 12 per cent in 20 years. Investment rates increased marginally from 16 per cent of GDP to 20 per cent, and improved only marginally to 21 per cent in the next decade. The share of exports and imports in the economy were similar at approx. 6.5 per cent, respectively. The overall trade to GDP ratio (a measure of economic openness) stood at 13.2 per cent in 1950–51. Owing to the inward-looking nature of the policies, within 20 years, trade fell to 7.2 per cent of GDP.

At the same time, other Asian countries were also undertaking their transformation. Take the example of South Korea. In 1960, India's and Korea's per capita incomes were not very different. In current dollars, India's per capita GDP stood at $90, while South Korea's incomes were $156. In the three decades since, by 1990, South Korea's incomes widened to $6,600, while Indian incomes stood at $367. The impact of the differing policies adopted is quite clear. Investments in South Korea increased from 10 per cent of GDP in 1960 to 39 per cent of GDP by 1990. Exports increased from 2.5 per cent of GDP to 25 per cent during the same time. South Korea averaged a real GDP growth rate of 9.6 per cent between 1960 and 1990. Per capita GDP, in turn, grew by 7.7 per cent in the same period. Considering the fact that around the time of Indian independence, per capita incomes (in purchasing power parity terms) in India and South Korea were broadly similar (South Korea's incomes were at $930, while India's at $985), the way South Korea grew for three decades transformed their economy completely. Granted, the population pressure and the geographical area of India are much larger, and the political structure different, but then, South Korea was not the only country either.

Taiwan (Republic of China) grew at a rate of 9.4 per cent between 1960 and 1990. Per capita income went from $153 to $7,663. Before South Korea, Japan, with per capita income of $2,700 after the Second World War, had seen a period of rapid growth through outward-looking policies, often referred to as the 'Japanese Miracle'. South Korea, Taiwan, Singapore and Hong Kong were together called the 'East Asian Tigers' for maintaining exceptionally high growth rates in per capita incomes and for transforming themselves within one generation. China more recently has been another success story built on internationally competitive manufacturing export industries. Between 1990 and 2010, it grew at an annual rate of close to 10 per cent, with per capita income growing at 9 per cent. Exports increased from 6 per cent of GDP to 27 per cent of GDP during this time. Export-promotion policies were crucial in the success stories of these countries. Public investments to boost connectivity were crucial and so were investments in human capital.

However, this is not to say that India should have copied the Korean model, or now copy the Chinese model. But it does hold important policy lessons, such as building private enterprise, integrating in global markets and the government playing the role of a facilitator of investments, growth and employment.

While it would be incorrect to suggest that these countries promoted free trade, an export orientation was nonetheless evident. Domestic industries were protected by tariff and non-tariff barriers, but foreign investments and technologies were welcome. The import regime for capital and intermediate goods was liberal, encouraging transfer of technology and final goods manufacturing. Gradually, domestic capabilities were built up in capital and intermediate goods as well, moving the industries of these countries up the value chain. Earnings from exports ensured forex reserves remained intact, allowing for competitive exchange rates as well.

On the domestic front, innovation and entrepreneurship were not shackled like they were in India. An enabling environment was created for domestic industry to thrive. Industries in these countries were able to achieve economies of scale in manufacturing, thereby becoming cost-competitive in global industries. These success stories are there for all to see. The Japanese automobile industry wrested control away from traditional American heavyweights such as General Motors and Ford. The Japanese and later Korean consumer goods industries continue to dominate the world. We all use Sony, Panasonic, Samsung or LG appliances in our households today. As the American economy transitioned from being a manufacturing powerhouse to a service-led economy, particularly tech and finance, the space ceded by them was occupied by these countries. It is through vibrant private enterprise that these countries were able to raise the government revenues necessary for investments in public infrastructure and human capital. Regulation, rather than control, allowed innovation and entrepreneurship to thrive, driving efficiency and competitiveness in global markets. In an era conducive to global trade and investment, India missed a huge opportunity in building a globally competitive manufacturing industry.

However, this is not to say that the early days of planning in India did not bring success. The focus of PM Nehru on science and technology education saw the Indian Institutes of Technology come up and have consistently provided world-class education to India's graduates. The prestigious Indian Institutes of Management (IIMs) also came up during this time. National Institutes of Technology and All India Institute of Medical Sciences are other major success stories. The Atomic Energy Commission is another. They continue to make important contributions to the development of not just the Indian but global economy now. Primary education was also expanded considerably during these times, as evidenced by rising literacy rates.

Early success was also seen in infrastructure projects, especially in dams, which Nehru saw as the 'temples of modern India'. These projects were not only large in scale but also engineering marvels in their own right, representing the new India of those times. Take the Bhakra-Nangal Dam for example. It was the second-highest dam in the world at the time and generated a million kilowatts of electricity and irrigated 7.5 million hectares of land.[18] Steel plants in Bhilai and Bokaro are other large-scale projects that were commissioned and made operational.

Achieving food security through the Green Revolution is another big success story of these times. The cooperative movement saw India becoming self-sufficient in milk. Credit goes to Dr Verghese Kurien, who was instrumental in the White Revolution, as a direct result of which India is now the world's largest producer of milk. Through Dr Kurien's interventions, millions of farmers were empowered. Amul is now an established brand in India, diversifying into value-added products such as chocolates and ice creams, among others. But perhaps, the greatest success has been the creation of institutions and structures for democracy to thrive in India.

Reforms by Stealth

The 1970s was a decade of political and economic turmoil, not just in India but globally too. Economic growth slowed considerably during this period. GDP growth slowed to 2.9 per cent, while per capita income growth slowed to 0.9 per cent. By 1979–80, investment rates had only increased marginally to 21 per cent of GDP from 20 per cent in 1969–70. The share of industry and manufacturing also saw marginal increases in this decade. The

[18]Guha, Ramachandra, *India After Gandhi: The History of the World's Largest Democracy*, Macmillan/Picador, London, 2007.

1970s saw growth and investment slow down even further.

However, several large real estate firms saw their origins around this time. The Shriram Group in Chennai was established in 1974. Apollo Tyres was incorporated in 1972 and they opened their first factory in Kerala in 1977. In 1976, Hindustan Computers Limited was formed and it introduced India's first personal computer (more commonly PC) in 1978.

Biocon was founded by Kiran Mazumdar-Shaw in 1978. A first-generation entrepreneur, she started manufacturing from the garage of her family home.[19] Navigating numerous challenges as an entrepreneur in the Licence Raj, Mazumdar-Shaw promoted a new field of biotechnology. She further had to overcome gender stereotypes, when many considered it uncommon for women to lead a business. Her early investments in R&D built competitive advantage during the initial stage of the company. Glenmark Pharmaceuticals was also established around the same time. However, these success stories were few and far between and wealth creation was still viewed with suspicion. Entrepreneurship was not a viable option for the masses even then.

By the 1980s, however, things began to change. Close to 30 years of import substitution policies, state-owned enterprises and extensive licencing and controls failed to show any discernible results. The success of East Asian economies and now, China, were starting to become more and more visible. It was increasingly recognized that export promotion and an open view to foreign trade and investment, along with extensive private sector involvement, would be crucial to any growth aspirations India had.

This era witnessed some elements of liberalization and growth picking up. Referred to as 'reform by stealth' by several authors, it witnessed many measures including loosening of

---

[19]Gopalakrishnan, R., and Sushmita Srivastava, *How Kiran Mazumdar-Shaw 'Fermented Biocon'*, Rupa Publications, New Delhi, 2020.

import controls and investments in telecom infrastructure and connectivity through the Centre for Development of Telematics (C-DOT) that had a wide-ranging impact on the economy. This is corroborated by evidence that growth rates spiked in the 1980s. From just 2.9 per cent annual growth in the 1970s, the 1980s saw the economy grow at 5.7 per cent. Per capita income grew at 3.6 per cent. This improved economic performance has been attributed to increased participation of private enterprise. Import controls were loosened. The OGL list for imports was expanded, meaning goods on this list were freely importable.

However, industrial licences were still required. As Panagariya notes, in 1976, the OGL list included 79 capital goods items, and by 1988, it covered 1,170 capital goods items and 949 intermediate inputs.[20] Perhaps crucially, these lists covered information technology (IT) equipment and computers, among others, promoting the computer revolution in India.

Some forms of export incentives were also introduced in this time. Some industrial controls too were beginning to be dismantled, particularly after 1985. Automatic licences for capacity expansion, depending on capacity utilization, raising of thresholds under the Monopolies and Restrictive Trade Practices (MRTP) Act, and price and distribution controls on cement and aluminium were removed. Reforms happened on the taxation front too. The first step to value-added tax (VAT), the precursor to the goods and services tax (GST), was taken in 1986 with the introduction of the Modified Value Added Tax system. Income tax rates were brought down.

Some seeds of India's private enterprise competitiveness can be traced to this era. Infosys was founded in 1981 by seven engineers who included N.R. Narayana Murthy and Nandan Nilekani. Wipro

---

[20]Panagariya, Arvind, 'India's Trade Reform', *India Policy Forum*, Vol. 1, p. 5, 2004.

entered the IT products business in 1982. In 1985–86, Sunil Bharti started manufacturing push-button telephones.

Maruti Suzuki was founded in 1981 by the GoI in partnership with Suzuki. This is a great example of public–private partnerships (PPP) in showing that the goals of national development and private development were not necessarily mutually exclusive. The automobile industry was forever changed with the introduction of the Maruti 800 in 1983, when Indian consumers had a choice between either Hindustan Motors' Ambassador or the Premier Padmini.

I recall when I was the district collector in the Malabar region of Kerala, my driver, Surendran, used to have a tough time manoeuvring the Ambassador on the narrow roads. In fact, throughout my journey in the civil service, I have only used the Ambassador. Only towards the end of my career did I get to experience the Maruti Ciaz, which was a refreshing change.

The launch of the Maruti 800 was aspirational, in tune with the dream of millions of owning a car. So not surprisingly, it remained India's highest selling car for two decades until it was discontinued. The Omni was launched in 1984, and the Gypsy in 1985. In 1984, Hero Honda, later Hero MotoCorp, was started as a joint venture between Honda and Hero Group. Titan Industries was created in 1987.

Another Crisis Brewing

However, this growth spurt was relatively short-lived, as the growth of the 1980s was fuelled by fiscal profligacy leading to a precarious macroeconomic position, as revealed by Montek Singh Ahluwalia.[21] India's combined fiscal deficit in the 1970s stood at 4.5

---

[21]Singh Ahluwalia, Montek, *Backstage: The Story Behind India's High Growth Years*, Rupa Publications, New Delhi, 2020.

per cent and in the 1980s, this doubled to 9–10 per cent. Shankar
Acharya, writing in 2017, echoed similar views to Ahluwalia.[22] This
was also a time when the Reserve Bank of India (RBI) 'monetized'
deficits of the government. This meant that to buy government
bonds, the RBI printed more money, increasing money supply.
Higher money supply, in turn, led to higher inflation and an
eroding value of the rupee. External debt took on a greater role
as well, exacerbating pressures. Inefficient public expenditure was
perhaps the other major factor. Subsidies and interest payments
formed a large chunk of government expenditures.

Public-sector enterprises, owing to outdated technology and
inefficient management, were not returning the sort of surpluses
as envisioned by successive governments. Leakages in public
expenditures were also rife. As a young collector in Kerala, I
recall PM Rajiv Gandhi stating that for every rupee spent by the
government, 85 paise were leaked, meaning that they did not
reach their intended beneficiaries.[23] A ballooning fiscal deficit
created excess demand in the economy, which spilled over into the
current account deficit, Ahluwalia recounts in his book *Backstage*.

Geopolitical affairs saw the price of oil spike again, with Iraq
invading Kuwait in 1990. Remittances, which had been a stable
stream of forex inflows, were also severely impacted, exacerbating
the situation. External financing started to dry up following a
worsening external position. Deposits by non-resident Indians
were being withdrawn. Clearly, there was a crisis of confidence
in the Indian economy during this time.

Looking back, it is clear that foreign exchange crises were a
constant feature in India's economic history post-Independence.

---

[22]Acharya, Shankar, 'Fiscal Deficits: A Short History', *Business Standard*, 8 March
2017, https://bit.ly/3nGjnPM, accessed on 6 July 2022.
[23]Saksena, Devendra, 'The 85-paise riddle!' *The Statesman*, 10 August 2017,
https://bit.ly/3xGPeVm, accessed on 20 June 2022.

Building competitiveness in exports and encouraging long-term FDI would have built a solid base on which to finance imports of capital and intermediate goods. Managing the exchange rate at fixed levels implied that in periods of outflows of forex, reserves had to be drawn down to maintain the value of the rupee. The episodes of 1956–57, devaluation in 1966 and other such events essentially built up to the major crisis of 1990–91.

While external events such as the Organization of Petroleum Exporting Countries declaring oil embargos spiked oil prices and triggered a global recession, India was fairly insulated from global trade and investment shocks at this point. The failure of monsoons and subsequent droughts impacted agriculture significantly. Again, this is more reflective of the failure of public investment in agriculture since the colonial times. Expenditures tilted towards subsidies, rather than investment. Political turmoil was also fairly common during this time, which some may blame for the poor economic performance. While it no doubt had an impact, the excessive control of the government over the economy meant that economic policy often responded to political considerations. The lack of a clear direction in policy and consequent outcomes is reflective of this. The economy went from crisis to crisis, doubling back on the flawed policies each time external crises reared their head.

The crisis of 1990–91 however laid bare the massive fissures in the Indian economy. Taping over these cracks, as was done before, would not be enough. Fortunately, this time around, we ushered in reforms that would change the face of the Indian economy forever.

THREE

TRYST WITH REFORMS

While the 1980s saw the gradual introduction of reforms, the need to make them wide ranging began to be felt. The voices calling for looser controls and a greater orientation towards global trade and investment were now drowning out the voices who still advocated inward-looking policies. For decades, India had been held back by the belief that looking inwards would be the solution to its development puzzle. However, data and global experiences were increasingly refuting this school of thought. The collapse of the Soviet Union and the rise of China based on outward-oriented policies shifted the dialogue towards economic liberalization and the benefits of globalization. China had made substantial inroads into manufacturing by the beginning of the 1990s. South Korea, Taiwan and the other East Asian Tigers had reached high-income status by now.

1991: Independence for the Economy

In India, on the other hand, reserves had dropped to precariously low levels. By April 1991, it only had reserves to pay for a few weeks of imports, when the norm is years. India had to pledge physical gold for loans. With another forex crisis looming on the horizon, India had no recourse but to seek external assistance from the International Monetary Fund and the World Bank. While these came with certain conditionalities, the ambitious reform agenda had more to do with domestic will and conviction than influence from multilaterals.

The first step in arresting the decline was a devaluation of the rupee. Cumulatively, a depreciation of 19 per cent was seen in two stages on 1 and 3 July. While a devaluation of the rupee stemmed immediate outflows, wide-ranging measures were taken in trade, industry and financial policies, among others. These reforms would form the bedrock of the high-growth years in the future.

Perhaps more importantly than unleashing growth in the future, these reforms changed the narrative around entrepreneurship, private enterprise and wealth creation.

In trade policy, import licencing was done away with. Exim scrips were introduced in July 1991, which would eliminate licencing for imports. Earlier, exporters were issued replenishment licences for their import requirements, Ahluwalia recounts in *Backstage*.[1] The new exim scrips would be earned at a uniform rate of 30 per cent of exports, and perhaps crucially, freely traded on the market. They also acted as a form of automatic stabilizers, as Ahluwalia explains. If the demand for imports exceeded the supply of scrips, then their prices in the market would increase, bringing down supply. This was an important step in moving away from control- to market-based determinants. What is interesting to note is the speed at which these trade reforms were carried out. In less than a day, India's trade policy stood transformed.

The other part was reducing import duties. Panagariya notes that the highest tariff rate in 1990–91 stood at 355 per cent and the average tariff rate was 113 per cent.[2] By 1993–94, the top rate had fallen to 85 per cent. This shows the extent to which trade was liberalized in India. Export controls were also gradually done away with, opening up more sectors for exports. The exchange rate was also moved from being fixed to flexible.

Perhaps more significantly, a liberalization of trade in services also occurred, which would prove to be a game changer for the Indian enterprise. Sectors such as telecommunications, civil aviation, banking and insurance were slowly opened up to private enterprise after the reforms of 1991. Liberalizing the FDI regime

[1]Singh Ahluwalia, Montek, *Backstage: The Story Behind India's High Growth Years*, Rupa Publications, New Delhi, 2020.
[2]Panagariya, Arvind, 'India's Trade Reform', *India Policy Forum*, Vol. 1, p. 7, 2004.

was another crucial reform on the external front. Apart from foreign capital and stable forex inflows, this reform would also bring with it the much-needed access to technology. Majority ownership of foreign entities was now allowed—a marked change from the regime that limited foreign ownership to 40 per cent in the 1970s. Multinationals started making a comeback in India. Procedures were simplified and an 'automatic' route created. For applications beyond this automatic route, the Foreign Investment Promotion Board (FIPB) was created to evaluate applications. Foreign institutional or portfolio investments were allowed to invest in Indian capital markets beginning 1992, in a series of capital market reforms.

The dismantling of the Licence Raj was the highlight of the reform agenda. The Industrial Policy Statement was laid in Parliament just a few hours before the then finance minister Dr Manmohan Singh presented his historic budget on 24 July 1991. All industrial controls were dismantled. The MRTP Act was diluted, enabling companies to grow. Essentially, the reforms of 1991 were industrial delicencing reforms.

The Budget presented by Dr Singh in 1991–92 laid out the rationale and the need for reforms. The Tax Reforms Committee under the chairmanship of Raja J. Chelliah and the Narasimham Committee were constituted. Both would propose wide-ranging reforms. Some of the big-ticket reform recommendations of the Chelliah committee included reducing personal and corporate income tax rates, reducing import duties and moving towards a VAT, among others. A crucial recommendation that was implemented was the abolition of wealth tax. Furthermore, the number of tax slabs of personal income was brought down from four to three in 1992–93. Personal income tax rates were brought down from a high of 56 per cent to 40 per cent by 1994–95. Taxation reforms continued and culminated in the Budget of 1997–98, which further reduced income tax rates to 10-20-30 per cent. Corporate taxes were reduced to 35 per cent.

These reforms would not have been possible without the tireless efforts of those who worked behind the scenes. A.N. Verma, principal secretary to the PM, played a crucial role. I had the privilege of working with Verma as a young officer and learnt much from him on how to drive change. His clarity of mind and conviction have always stood out to me. As Rakesh Mohan recounts, Verma, in his earlier capacity as industry secretary, had already laid much of the groundwork for the industrial policy reforms of 1991.[3] Ahluwalia, too, played a key role as commerce secretary. I had the pleasure of working with him, and he always stood out as a man with immense clarity of mind. No doubt, there are many others who played crucial roles behind the scenes. The political leadership of the time also deserves a lot of credit for building a political consensus around the reforms.

IT and ITeS: The Poster Child of Liberalization

A direct consequence of the economic reforms was the boom in India's software industry. While the seeds of competitiveness were sown in the late 1970s and early 1980s, it is only post economic reforms that these companies became global giants. From $100-million revenue in 1990, the software industry brought home revenues of $1 billion by 1996, Kris S. Gopalakrishnan, one of the founders of Infosys, informs us.[4]

---

[3]Mohan, Rakesh, 'Introduction: The Road to the 1991 Industrial Policy Reforms and Beyond: A Personalised Narrative from the Trenches', *India Transformed: 25 Years of Economic Reforms*, Rakesh Mohan (ed.), Penguin Random House India, New Delhi, 2017.

[4]Gopalakrishnan, Kris S., 'Indian IT and ITeS Journey: Liberalization and Beyond', *Mint*, 26 April 2016, https://bit.ly/3RhtzvF, accessed on 7 July 2022.

In fact, the story of Infosys is perhaps synonymous with India's software boom. Recounting to Vedica Kant, management consultant, author and historian, in an interview, Narayana Murthy recalled how tough it really was for Infosys.[5] It took years to get a telephone connection. Banks did not understand the concept of software and required tangible collateral. By the time Infosys won its first contract, they did not even have enough money to buy their first computer. By offering on-site services to clients and paying an Indian salary to engineers, Infosys was able to negotiate advances with discounts to incentivize advance payments. This is how they were able to get the clients to finance their business. More international contracts followed and by 1987, it had set up offices in the United States (US), one on each coast.

The legendary former CEO of General Electric (GE), Jack Welch's visit to India in 1989 proved to be a seminal moment for the Indian IT industry. This is around the same time that the business process outsourcing (BPO) industry saw its genesis. General Electric and American Express were pioneers in this space. As Nilekani explained, working with a leading global company made Infosys think differently and ultimately played a key role in its global expansion. In 1990, Software Technology Parks (STPs) were promoted by the Ministry of Electronics and Information Technology. These played a crucial role in the development of India's IT industry. Here, an enabling environment was created for industry to grow. The STPs provided plug-and-play facilities and high-speed connectivity along with export benefits to help foster growth in this industry. India's success in STPs can be thought of as analogous to China's success with large-scale special economic zones (SEZs) in manufacturing.

Here, N. Vittal, the then secretary in the Department of

---

[5]Kant, Vedica, 'Source Code', *FiftyTwo.in.*, 24 September 2021, https://bit.ly/3P6gCTG, accessed on 7 July 2022.

Electronics, deserves much credit for the development of India's IT industry. He was quick to recognize the potential of the sector and drove through important reforms and initiatives that led to the development of the IT story. I frequently interacted with him when he was chairman of the Central Vigilance Commission. I believe this posting was a waste of a man who was very development oriented. I always felt he could have delivered 10 times more for the country had he continued to work in the IT sector. Vittal's experience is indeed one of the tragedies of government. Officers with in-depth knowledge are usually not afforded long innings in their fields of specialization. As a result, officers are unable to specialize and gain extensive domain knowledge. This sort of continuity and experience is crucial in building competitive industries.

While government policies promoted growth, the process was entirely private enterprise led. Striving for excellence and embracing the quality movement were crucial to the growth of industry as well, Kris Gopalakrishnan notes.[6] This contributed to competitiveness in global markets. Enabling foreign investment with 100 per cent ownership also created competition in the markets, making Indian enterprises more efficient and productive. Rather than protecting Indian industry, opening it up to competition on a level playing field made it thrive. The sector saw a steady stream of incoming graduates, trained through India's technical education system. This is another example of the public and private sector working together to achieve shared national objectives. The success of this industry demonstrated that new enterprises could thrive if an enabling environment for their success is created.

Closely related is the success in the telecommunications space, which played an enabling role in the development of the software

---

[6]Gopalakrishnan, Kris S., 'Indian IT and ITeS Journey: Liberalization and Beyond', *Mint*, 26 April 2016, https://bit.ly/3RhtzvF, accessed on 7 July 2022.

industry. The National Telecom Policy was announced in 1994. Sunil Bharti, who was in the business of manufacturing phones at the time, successfully bid for one of the licences in Delhi, where he launched cellular services under the brand Airtel. A gutsy entrepreneur, he has the courage and determination to constantly innovate in the face of market and regulatory disruptions.

While the 1994 policy has been considered to be ineffective, it did set the ball rolling for private enterprise-led development of this space. Tariffs were set at prohibitively high rates, making mobile phones the domain of the rich. This is because of the high licence fees private operators had to pay. However, it was soon recognized that a new policy would be needed. A level playing field was required. Changes were made with the establishment of the Telecom Regulatory Authority of India (TRAI) in 1997. The New Telecom Policy, 1999, made further changes. Here, revenue-sharing mechanisms, rather than licence fees were introduced. TRAI became a policy advisory body on issues such as granting of new licences and tariffs. A separate tribunal was created to manage disputes. A new department of telecommunications was created and Bharat Sanchar Nigam Limited and Mahanagar Telephone Nigam Limited were corporatized.

Again, while this sector has seen significant churn and consolidation, it is no doubt that the proliferation of mobile data and connectivity has primarily been a private enterprise-led effort. The software and BPO booms in India were enabled by reforms in telecommunications, as this democratized the availability of international lines, internet lines, etc.

A Transformed Financial Sector

Financial services, too, received a huge fillip from the reforms, particularly the Narasimham Committee, which submitted its report in 1992. The committee suggested reforms that went on to alter the face of the Indian banking system. Reductions in the statutory liquidity ratio (SLR) and the cash reserve ratio (CRR) were recommended. High levels of SLR meant that banks had to keep a high proportion of their assets in government securities. A high CRR meant that banks had to keep a high fraction of their deposits as reserves. A high SLR crowded out private credit requirements, while a high CRR inhibited credit creation.

Banks were also given more freedom in pricing their loans, based on the risk profile. This created stronger credit markets. Crucially, new licences for private-sector banks were granted. HDFC Bank, ICICI Bank and IndusInd Bank are among the ones granted licences back then. Now, the former two are among India's largest banks.

The Narasimham Committee also called for a dilution of holdings in public-sector banks (PSBs), which allowed them to dip into capital markets to raise funds as well. The private banks were quick to leverage technology in their operations, which gave them an advantage over PSBs, which were slow to modernize. Competition from the private sector drove home the point that without adopting technology, the PSBs would be left behind.

The Securities and Exchange Board of India (SEBI) was set up in 1992. Private-sector mutual funds would now compete with the Unit Trust of India (UTI). Innovations in the financial sector had a knock-on effect on the rest of the economy as well. For instance, a robust market for consumer durable finance and housing finance emerged on the backs of rising incomes. This fuelled consumption and drove industrial and construction growth. In turn, employment was increased in these industries, which further drove consumption growth. The insurance sector was also gradually de-monopolized, deregulated and opened up to private and foreign investment. The much-needed transparency and accountability were also brought in to India's capital markets.

However, when the nation was rocked by the infamous Harshad Mehta scam of 1992—the room for which was created by the absence of digitization of security exchanges—the need to rebuild trust was felt.

Many would not remember, but the computerization movement in India was not without its dissidents across a range of industries, including banking and finance. I have seen this evolution from the time it was opposed by the communists in Kerala to the Communist Party of India (Marxist) computerizing its own offices![7]

Even though bank unions had been opposing computerization, the process was accelerated following this scam. The National Stock Exchange (NSE) was established in 1992, with fully automated exchanges and electronic matching. The NSE enabled qualified dealers to trade from anywhere using computers and leased lines. The Bombay Stock Exchange (BSE), which had been resisting computerization, accelerated the adoption of technology in the face of competition from the NSE. Another spillover effect of the establishment of the NSE was that it attracted foreign portfolio investment, which had also been allowed as part of the reform package. The National Securities Depository Limited was established in 1996, further strengthening India's equity markets. Both the public and private sector had a leading role to play in these developments. HDFC Bank and SBI were early promoters, along with the Industrial Development Bank of India (IDBI), UTI and the NSE.

---

[7]Babu, Ramesh, 'Ahead of Meet, Debate on Ideological Shift Rages in Kerala CPI(M)', *Hindustan Times*, 28 March 2022, https://bit.ly/3x7JT9X, accessed on 8 September 2022.

Industry and Infrastructure Redefined

Automobile manufacturing is another success story of this time. At the time of reforms, Maruti, Hindustan Motors and Premier were in the prime position in the market. In the years following reforms, global giants such as Toyota, Honda and Hyundai, among others, set up manufacturing facilities in India. Just like in the case of the software sector, these companies brought with them the sophistication of their operations, technology and management practices that Indian enterprises had yet to see. This forced Indian companies to adapt. The effects were not just limited to the production majors. A large network of original equipment manufacturers (OEMs) also thrived in response to the unlocking of the industry. These were mostly small and medium enterprises (SMEs) that grew and upgraded their technology as well. Owning a car was not just a luxury now. The emerging middle class created demand on a scale not seen before.

The pharmaceutical sector also benefitted from the dismantling of the Licence Raj and the opening up to foreign trade and investment. In 1994, the reform agenda was extended to the pharmaceutical sector, through the Modification in Drug Policy, 1986, resulting in an explosion of domestic manufacturing. Sun Pharma, established in 1983, listed on the stock exchange in 1994, while Divi's Laboratories entered the manufacturing space in 1990.

The reform agenda of 1991 saw the list of industries reserved for the public sector down from 18 to just six. This kick-started private operations in industries such as steel, telecom and refining, among others. While intermediate and capital good industries had been liberalized in 1991, it took some time to liberalize consumer goods industries, with gradualism in consumer goods preferred. Licences were still required, and in many cases, imports were altogether banned. The manufacturing of many consumer goods was still reserved for small-scale industries until 1997. It was only in 2000, when the World Trade Organization ruled against India, that consumer goods imports were liberalized.

However, the reforms did change the perception of consumerism in India. Coming from an era of shortages, the sheer increase in choices was baffling for those who had grown up in the age of price and quantity controls. Consequently, India's consumer goods industry started to evolve during this time as well, as exemplified by Marico Industries, which was founded by Harsh Mariwala. A second-generation entrepreneur, Harsh joined the family business in 1971. After popularizing Parachute as a household name in the domestic coconut oil industry, Marico was set up in 1990. Now, it is a household name in India's fast-moving consumer goods (FMCG) industry. I was delighted to learn about the fascinating story behind Marico. I have always admired Harsh as a driver of innovation through the Marico Innovation Foundation, where he supports young entrepreneurs.

Incumbents such as ITC and HUL were able to adapt to the changing reality and weather global competition. Godrej maintained competitiveness in a few industries as well by maintaining their specialization. The group has played an important role in building India's manufacturing capabilities.

While some Indian companies were able to compete in the FMCG segment, the consumer durables segment was perhaps won by foreign companies. In the early 1990s, Indian brands such as Onida, Videocon and BPL, which made consumer goods such as televisions, fell out of favour with customers. International brands, such as Sony, LG and Samsung, saw an exponential increase in popularity too. Air conditioners, considered a luxury till the early 1990s, saw an explosion in demand, both due to rising incomes and falling prices. In this industry, however, we see Indian companies do well. Brands such as Voltas and Bluestar are household names today.

The infrastructure sector, too, was opened up to private enterprise participation. The first traces of PPP in infrastructure were seen in the power sector but failed to meet their objectives. However, a sector where PPPs have proven to be successful is roads and highways. The National Highways Act, 1956, was amended in 1995 to encourage private sector participation. However, as part of the continuing reform agenda, the biggest shift came in 1997 with the incorporation of the Infrastructure Development Finance Company (IDFC).[8] The Mumbai and Delhi airports were handed over to private management in the mid-2000s through a bidding process, and are now the finest airports in India, with the potential to emerge as global aviation hubs.

The PPP projects expanded to the point where India became one of the largest PPP markets in the world. Several enabling mechanisms contributed to the development of PPP markets in India. First, the government set up a special cell in the Department of Economic Affairs (DEA) for streamlining PPP approvals. Furthermore, the viability gap funding scheme supported the financial viability of these projects. Standardization of documents and a pipeline of bankable PPP projects, among others, were steps taken by the DEA and the Planning Commission to popularize PPPs in India. The Infrastructure Vertical in the Planning Commission did path-breaking work to provide impetus to PPP projects. This helped change mindsets in departments which were accustomed to item-wise and EPC (engineering, procurement and construction) contracts.

Civil aviation was also opened up to the private sector. Earlier, the private sector would only be allowed in the chartered flights segment. Within a few years, from just having one international and one domestic carrier, Air India and Indian Airlines, respectively,

---

[8]Chatterjee, Vinayak, 'PPP in India: The Story So Far', *Business Standard*, 21 January 2013, https://bit.ly/3bK9cHh, accessed on 7 July 2022.

both PSEs, new airlines sprung up. Jet Airways and Air Sahara are a few early examples followed by IndiGo, Vistara, GoAir (now Go First) and SpiceJet in the new millennium, which are now leading the way in India's civil aviation industry. Air India is now a private entity as well. While there has been significant churn and consolidation in the sector, the development of India's civil aviation industry has been a private sector-led affair. The development of airports and the building of new ones were also undertaken in partnership with the private sector. Starting with the Delhi and Mumbai airports, the Bengaluru and Hyderabad airports are other examples of privately managed airports in India. The effects of private management were clear within a few years. These are now world-class airports, offering amenities and services at par with the global best. Kerala developed the Cochin airport as a greenfield project and expanded the runway of Calicut Airport through financing by NRIs.

In 2018, a fourth airport was inaugurated in Kannur in northern Kerala, making it the only state then with four international airports. These airports have been the biggest catalysts in the emergence of the state as a unique travel and tourism brand.

Carriers such as IndiGo were key in connecting new markets within India. While domestic connectivity was led by Indian companies, they were unable to gain a foothold in international markets. This was owing to a variety of factors, including regulatory and financial issues. A lot of routes were catered to by international carriers, like Emirates and Qatar, making their airports hubs of wealth creation. We must recognize the same in India. It is necessary that the airports at Delhi, Mumbai, Bangalore and Hyderabad and the upcoming airport at Noida emerge as international hubs. I hope that railway stations go the way of airports in the future. The proposal to hand over management of railway stations to the private sector can create world-class stations and unlock their latent economic potential, leading the process of smart urbanization.

Scaling Through Low-Cost Innovations

In independent India, private enterprise was largely driven by the traditional large business houses. However, while these business houses consolidated and expanded their operations, and new business opportunities were created post-Independence, the systems of controls and licences discouraged new entrepreneurs from entering the market. Entrepreneurs who would disrupt industries and change the rules of the game were few and far between. Dhirubhai Ambani, J.R.D. Tata and Ghanshyam Das Birla were some of the early entrepreneurs who left a lasting mark on India.

Even though India had set up several institutes such as the IIMs to promote business education, the absence of entrepreneurs sprouting from these institutes was peculiar, according to Dwijendra Tripathi.[9] Innovation and R&D were also low on the agenda for Indian corporates during this time. Protected against domestic competition, the quality of products suffered. The large technological deficit meant that Indian companies often partnered with foreign companies, rather than innovating or acquiring new technologies. The management structure of Indian companies barely changed even after Independence. Both ownership and management remained within the hands of the family or extended family. Professional management of family-owned enterprises was rare.

The opening up of the economy created new career paths and opportunities. First, the direct effect of the success of India's software firms triggered a shift in perceptions in regard to entrepreneurship.

---

[9]Tripathi, Dwijendra, *The Oxford History of Indian Business*, Oxford University Press, India, 2004.

The success of software companies signalled a change in culture and aspirations. No longer were Indians interested in safe jobs. They struck out on their own. Entrepreneurship and wealth creation were no longer looked down upon. Nilekani writes that an early effect of the software industry was in altering the culture of India's business and entrepreneurship.[10] He goes on to explain why. First, serving export markets meant that global management practices and standards were adopted by Indian companies. This perhaps proved crucial in achieving a global footprint by Indian firms. Companies were now investing more than ever before in employees, upgrading their skills and promoting constant learning. Second, companies such as Infosys showed that it was possible for those without a business background to succeed as entrepreneurs. Earlier, it was the traditional communities which had been involved in trade and commerce for thousands of years that made up a large chunk of India's private enterprise. An article published in 1994 captures the flavour of the time.[11] It notes that not only was skilled manpower important but so were entrepreneurial skills. Indian companies soon developed a reputation of delivering quality, customized software.

Family businesses, the cornerstone of Indian enterprise were also galvanized, writes Gita Piramal.[12] According to her, close to 6,000 new companies were started between 1992 and 1996 by various family groups. This expansion was also accompanied by a diversification of interests by the most entrepreneurial.

---

[10]Nilekani, Nandan, *Imagining India: The Idea of a Renewed Nation*, Penguin Books, 2010.

[11]Sharma, Pranjal, 'CHIPS of Success', *India Today*, 31 May 1994, https://bit.ly/3yN7AFK, accessed on 7 July 2022.

[12]Piramal, Gita, 'Animal Spirits: Stray Thoughts on the Nature of Entrepreneurship in India's Business Families After Liberalisation', *India Transformed: 25 Years of Economic Reforms*, Rakesh Mohan (ed.), Penguin Random House India, New Delhi, 2017.

Analysing the period between 1990 and 2016, she finds that family businesses increasingly moved into knowledge-based businesses and consumer-facing companies—a sharp turn from the traditional agriculture-based industries such as cotton, sugar and tea that they were involved in earlier.

We also see considerable churn here. Close to 72 per cent of the top business families in India before 1990 fell out top-50 by 2016. First-generation entrepreneurs made up close to one-third of the list by 2016. This again demonstrates the impact of economic reforms on entrepreneurship. The entrepreneurs who were able to best adapt to the new reality and build their competitiveness, thrived, while the ones who could not, perished. There are stories of numerous second- and third-generation entrepreneurs, such as Harsh Mariwala, breaking away from their traditional family businesses and developing new ventures. Adaptability is a trait of entrepreneurs that is often the key differentiator of success. Many of the Indian entrepreneurs of the time neither came from big business families nor had large financial backing. They had to rely on their capabilities and skills to succeed in this world. This is exemplified by *jugaad*, or frugal innovation, defined as an 'innovative fix, an improvised solution born from ingenuity and cleverness' by Navi Radjou, Jaideep Prabhu and Simone Ahuja.[13]

A BBC feature highlighted India's frugal innovations.[14] A good example would be the famous dabbawallahs of Mumbai, known for their legendary reliability. Their model was studied by FedEx, Amazon and even Richard Branson of Virgin Atlantic. And these certainly were not new innovations. The system had

---

[13]Radjou, Navi, et al., *Jugaad Innovation: A Frugal and Flexible Approach to Innovation for the 21st Century*, Penguin Random House India, 2012.
[14]Koch, Christian, 'India's Ingenious Approach to Life', BBC | Travel, 3 September 2018, https://bbc.in/3ORSHYj, accessed on 7 July 2022.

been functioning for over a hundred years and documented to be one of the most efficient logistics networks in the world. There are many other such examples of frugal innovation. The BBC feature also talks about Kannan Lakshminarayan, a Chennai-based entrepreneur who developed an ATM—Gramateller ATM—for rural India that used a fraction of the electricity and cost a fraction of the money to install. Another great example is India's Mangalyaan mission. It cost a small fraction of most space launches, at $75 million only. Reusing parts, conducting ground tests and other interventions helped keep costs low. Mangalyaan made India the first Asian country to reach Mars. Mitticool, a clay fridge developed in the aftermath of the 2001 Gujarat earthquake, is another noteworthy innovation.

Indian entrepreneurs were quick to incorporate jugaad in their business models. The telecom sector is one example that has arguably adopted similar principles.[15] Installing telecom infrastructure was a huge capital expenditure, the funds for which many companies did not necessarily possess. Sunil Bharti recounts the roll-out of Airtel in Delhi in *India Transfromed*.[16] The network equipment required a large capital investment. He was able to convince Ericsson that initially, Airtel would pay a fraction of the cost upfront and the rest after the roll-out of the network. Going on, he notes that,

> The need to cater to India's unique market condition required
> them to be creative with their products and processes. They
> had to create/adapt products to Indian tastes and preferences,

---

[15]Ojha, Nikhil Prasad, and Dinkar Ayilavarapu, 'Leapfrogging the World with Frugal Innovation', *Mint*, 7 June 2016, https://bit.ly/3yN7ePq, accessed on 7 July 2022.
[16]Mittal, Sunil Bharti, 'Rise of the New Entrepreneurial Classes and the Emergence of a High-Growth Economy', *India Transformed: 25 Years of Economic Reforms*, Rakesh Mohan (ed.), Penguin Random House India, New Delhi, 2017.

and more importantly, bring them within the reach of the Indian 'buying power' through appropriate innovation and engineering.

Airtel's outsourcing business model, where network management and IT processes were outsourced, was unprecedented. This allowed Airtel to focus its resources on customer care and marketing. They partnered with global leaders such as Nokia and Ericsson to manage networks and ensure reliable service. IBM was partnered with to provide and manage IT equipment. Payments, in turn, were linked to revenues. So, Airtel could focus on growth, while not incurring massive capital expenditures. This would prove pivotal. Soon, this model became a global standard.

Similarly, Indian enterprises and entrepreneurs in the telecom field got together to expand network roll-out. This was achieved through 'passive infrastructure sharing', which meant that companies were sharing their network infrastructure. This is another example of innovative thinking by Indian entrepreneurs, overcoming barriers to entry and thriving by growing together. Furthermore, take the instance of Unilever adopting marketing practices evolved in India to the developed world.[17] The sachets of shampoos, small packs of detergent, etc., were innovations specific to the Indian market that went global. Liberalization and globalization brought to the fore the concept of frugal innovation or jugaad that was commonplace with India's entrepreneurs. Management literature on the same subject exploded, and jugaad was mainstreamed in the discourse.

---

[17]Vijayraghavan, Kala, 'Unilever Takes HUL Strategies Like Small Packs, Cheaper Variants to Developed Markets', *The Economic Times*, 28 September 2012, https://bit.ly/3bWcI1B, accessed on 7 July 2022.

The Unfinished Agenda

While the reforms of the early 1990s were wide-ranging and changed the face of India's economic trajectory, certain areas including labour laws, insolvency and bankruptcy, starting a new business and agriculture were left out of the agenda, either owing to political compulsions or other necessities. These legacy issues continued to act as a drag on economic growth. Had the reform agenda been fully implemented within the first 15 years, India's per capita income would have been closer to China's today.

The remnants of the old system could still most significantly be seen in the case of public-sector enterprises or undertakings (PSE/PSUs). In the reform agenda of 1991, privatization of PSUs had not yet entered the lexicon, mainly owing to political considerations. However, there was a clear recognition that the PSUs were not generating the sort of surpluses envisioned. In the face of fiscal consolidation, their functioning needed to be made more efficient and productive.

Perhaps, importantly, the 1991 agenda reduced the list of industries reserved for the public sector. At most, the public sector diluted their holdings in PSUs, in most cases less than 20 per cent; there were no changes to their functioning. These PSUs being owned by the government functioned more like departments when it came to flexibility and profit orientation. After all, if these companies functioned effectively, transferring large resources back to the government, then the fiscal and external situation would have been far less precarious. However, with limited flexibility afforded to managers and the bureaucratic nature of operations that had crept in, PSU reform was one area left untouched by the 1991 reform agenda.

Since then, however, we do see an increasing acceptance of PSU reform. A step forward was taken with the formation of the

Disinvestment Commission in 1996. In 1999, the Department of Disinvestment (later renamed Ministry of Disinvestment) was formed to oversee the process of disinvestment. This is around the time when 'privatization' entered our lexicon. Here, the process picked up significant pace. The Bharat Aluminium Company and Hindustan Zinc Ltd were sold to Vedanta. Suzuki bought a controlling stake in Maruti Suzuki. Videsh Sanchar Nigam Limited was sold to the Tata Group and Indian Petrochemicals Corporation Limited was bought by Reliance Industries. Several government-owned hotel properties were also sold during this time. Attempts were made to disinvest Bharat Petroleum Corporation Limited and Hindustan Petroleum Corporation Limited; however, these attempts were thwarted. The disinvestment agenda, nonetheless, slowed down considerably post 2004.

Labour reforms were also left out during the 1991 agenda. These labour laws, along with other laws, such as the MRTP Act, reservation for small-scale industries and the associated definition of small-scale operations kept Indian enterprise small at a time when manufacturing behemoths were coming up in East and Southeast Asia. While liberalizing imports for capital and intermediate goods no doubt improved competitiveness, the inability to build industries at scale meant we lost out on lucrative export markets.

By conventional wisdom, India had all the ingredients or 'factor endowments', as economists call it, to succeed in labour-intensive manufacturing industries. The conventional path of economic transformation tells us that as an economy develops, its composition moves from agriculture to manufacturing to services. However, the same was not true for India, even after the economic reforms. While product markets were liberalized, factor markets were not. Labour laws remained in place, with a gradual approach being preferred. This discouraged scale in manufacturing, something

China and other Asian countries were able to create successfully. The lack of large-scale job creation in manufacturing meant that labour was not pulled out of agriculture at a fast-enough pace for our per capita income to rise even further.

Land acquisition remained cumbersome and tied up in approvals and processes. Power supply was erratic and power tariffs were designed in a way that industrial tariffs were cross subsidizing consumer tariffs. Insufficient investment in infrastructure also impacted the competitiveness of our manufacturing enterprises. Our cost of logistics remained higher than most competing nations, further eroding any competitive advantage.

This dual approach—wide-ranging reforms in some areas along with vestiges of the past in others—allowed the economy to move forward at two speeds. Consequently, the high-growth sectors, such as IT, finance, professional services and others, grew exponentially. These firms were globally competitive and ready to fend off any competitive pressures. The same was however not true in manufacturing. Despite economic reforms liberalizing capital and intermediate goods, manufacturing industries failed to show any appreciable expansion. For instance, the share of manufacturing in GDP stood at approx. 15 per cent in 1991. By 2016, 25 years after the reforms, the share was alike.[18] A similar story emerges in employment. The shares of manufacturing in employment have remained stagnant as well, indicating that over 25 years, there has not been the sort of job creation in manufacturing as development theory had suggested. Employment in services expanded considerably, especially in skilled positions.

However, with a large chunk of our population still engaged in agriculture, our per capita income grew at a slower rate than China. For instance, in 1991, our per capita income stood at $303

---

[18]'World Development Indicators', The World Bank, https://bit.ly/2XIV9sO, accessed on 7 July 2022.

and that of China at $333.[19] By 2016, China's income accelerated to $8,000 per capita, while India's grew to $1,730. In real terms, income in China grew at 9 per cent per annum during this time, and Indian income at 5 per cent. This illustrates the difference between the growth stories of these two nations. On the back of a strong manufacturing sector, China ushered in a massive transformation. Our capabilities in manufacturing were surpassed by China, and an opportunity to integrate ourselves in global GVCs was lost.

❧

---

[19]'GDP per capita (current US$)', The World Bank, https://bit.ly/3AxW4iX, accessed on 7 July 2022.

FOUR

THE WORLD,
INDIA INC.'S OYSTER

By the turn of the millennium, a new India began to emerge. The economic reforms had firmly taken hold. Globalization became a buzzword. Within just 10 years, India's story was completely different from what it would have been. People started to talk of India's growth story. We were developing as a hub at the forefront of knowledge-intensive industries. Global investments started to pour in. Exports, especially in services, expanded like never before. Indian industries had built a reputation of reliability and quality. Domestic firms, initially sheltered from foreign competition, innovated and entered new business areas. First-generation entrepreneurs built some of the behemoths we see today.

The upward mobility offered by increased economic opportunities meant that millions of new households constituted a sizeable middle class in India now. Multinationals realized the scale of the markets that this burgeoning middle class had to offer. Apart from entrepreneurship, new jobs being created in fields such as software development, hospitality, retail, finance and consulting, among others, meant that the youth had plenty of career opportunities to choose from. And they were increasingly connected to the global world. Private television channels broadcast both domestic and international content. The introduction of mobile phones and the internet further connected Indians both to each other and internationally. The internet gave rise to opportunities in e-commerce, among many other areas.

In the immediate years following the reforms, growth did not pick up significantly. The average decadal growth rates in the 1980s and 1990s, were similar, just shy of 6 per cent.[1] However, there is an important differentiator between these two eras. Fiscal profligacy saw growth rates surge, especially in the late 1980s. However, this profligacy ultimately contributed to the crisis of 1991.

---

[1]National Accounts Statistics Back-Series for 2011-12.

Growth fell to 1.1 per cent in 1991–92 as a result of this crisis.

Growth started picking up after a period, largely driven by the private sector. The years between 1994 and 1997 saw growth rates average 7.3 per cent a year. However, the Asian financial crisis of 1997–98 saw growth take a hit. Despite most Southeast Asian economies suffering from this crisis, India was able to cushion the fall due to a steady build-up of reserves. By the end of the millennium, growth picked up to 8.8 per cent. The impact of liberalizing trade meant that the share of exports gradually grew from 6 per cent of GDP in 1990 to 10 per cent in 2000. Imports rose from similar levels to 13 per cent. By 2000, investment rates had risen to 24 per cent from 18–20 per cent in the post-Independence era.

However, in the first few years of the new millennium, growth stagnated. Agricultural production suffered in 1999 and 2000, with drought-like conditions persisting in several districts. Around the same time, the global economy was plunged into a recession. The dot-com bubble, which saw tech valuations sore, burst in March 2000. Markets plummeted and there was an official recession lasting up until 2001. This, too, had a bearing on India's growth prospects.

While the growth rates will obviously differ depending on which base we use, there is no denying that 2003 to 2010 were high-growth years, regarded by many as years of 'golden growth'. During this period, India posted some of the highest growth rates seen in the world, second only to China. Investment rates rose to above 30 per cent of GDP. Exports grew from 10 per cent of GDP in 2000 to 23 per cent of GDP by 2008–09. Imports, however, grew at a faster pace, reaching the level of 28 per cent of GDP. This was the start of an upward trajectory for the decade.

Global conviction in India's growth story was growing, leading to Goldman Sachs economist Jim O'Neill introducing the acronym

BRIC (Brazil, Russia, India and China) to denote a group of fast-growing, developing countries.

What perhaps differentiates this period from earlier periods of growth is that this time, the process was driven by the private sector, with the public sector playing an enabling role. There were important policy lessons from the growth of the new industries, such as software and BPO. Light touch regulation, combined with an enabling environment, through provision of infrastructure, common facilities, SEZs, tax benefits, etc., had a huge role to play in the development of these industries. Enabling policies also attracted foreign investment. Foreign firms entered India either through partnerships or directly. This increased competition in markets brought new technologies, processes and management culture.

Global Powerhouses

A liberalized, growing economy also led to an increase in foreign investments in India. Unstable and insufficient inflows of FDI were one of the reasons why we flittered from one forex crisis to another. Our focus was on controlling the outflow of forex, rather than encouraging their inflows. Now, through a policy environment enabling inflows, forex continued to pour in, building our reserves and stability. Overall macroeconomic stability is perhaps one of the most important precursors to sustained growth.

In 1991, total FDI in India stood at about $100 million. By 2000, this number had increased to $2 billion, a 20-time increase in just a decade. This trend continued. However, the years between 2008 and 2012 saw inflows moderated owing to the global financial crisis and subsequent great recession. Domestic conditions were also not as conducive to foreign investments as they had been in the earlier years.

By March 2014, annual FDI had fallen to $36 billion. Since

then, we see a steady increase in FDI again owing to favourable domestic policies. In 2020–21, the financial year most impacted by the Covid-19 pandemic, FDI inflows touched record levels of $81 billion. Reflecting India's strengths in the services sector, the highest percentage of FDI inflows were seen here. Since 2000, close to 30 per cent of India's cumulative FDI inflows have been in computer software, hardware, finance, banking, insurance, professional services, R&D and outsourcing, among others. The automobile sector, construction and telecommunications sector were others that received substantial inflows of FDI.

These figures are not surprising. Indian software companies such as Wipro, Infosys and TCS were beginning to dominate the global stage. The BPO industry thrived during these times, making India one of the leading service providers in the world. Gradually, India built on these capabilities and established a significant presence in knowledge process outsourcing (KPO) and information technology outsourcing. Foreign companies such as Microsoft, Google, IBM, Cisco, Adobe and Facebook, among numerous others, set up R&D centres in India during these times. Today, Indian companies such as Zoho Corp are building world-class products.

There were several benefits in opening up to FDI. First was the transfer of technology. India had so far lagged behind in technology in most sectors, barring a few such as software, ITeS (Information Technology-Enabled Services), etc. However, the gap was most prevalent in the manufacturing or industrial sector. The automobile and two-wheeler industries are pertinent examples. Initially, domestic manufacturers had partnered with foreign firms for technology, know-how, etc., either through joint ventures (JVs) or through other forms of partnership. In two-wheelers, the Hero Honda brand was increasingly popular. Bajaj, in partnership with Kawasaki, rolled out several products as well. Choices exploded for consumers, and brands were now competing. Both Indian brands eventually decided to go it alone and maintain a dominant position, not just in domestic markets but in global markets as well. They have played a pivotal role in developing India's two-wheeler industry and the ecosystem around it. Maruti Suzuki is another example in the passenger vehicle segment. German giants such as Mercedes started assembling cars locally, gradually expanding their facilities.

This sophistication in technology and operations had a knock-on effect on the entire value chain, right from OEMs to dealerships. The SMEs supplying parts and services to these industries also grew in their operations and sophistication to continue serving these large domestic and multinational firms. The entire value chain prospered.

Another key benefit of FDI was that Indian entrepreneurs, managers and firms were exposed to global management practices and processes. This further enhanced productivity and efficiency of operations. However, it was a two-way exchange. The Indian partners often provided the foreign partner crucial market information and inputs in product development, keeping in mind the nuances of the Indian markets. Competition also increased in domestic markets as a result of foreign entrants. This provided consumers more choices.

Indian companies not only weathered global competition but took to surpass it. During this era, there was a spate of mergers and acquisitions (M&As) made by large Indian enterprises not just domestically but also internationally. Indian companies were now acquiring firms not just in developing markets but developed markets as well. In fact, most outward investments from Indian firms went to developed markets. This reflected India's new image at the turn of the millennium. India had arrived on the global stage and was here to stay.

The Tata Group was at the forefront here. In 2000, the 180-year-old Tetley Tea was acquired by Tata Tea. Impressively, the value of the deal was three times that of Tata Tea itself, reflecting the ambition. This deal helped catapult Tata Tea into a major global player. Similarly, Tata Steel bought the Anglo-Dutch steelmaker Corus for nearly $13 billion in 2007, again making Tata Steel among the biggest steel producers in the world. Tata Motors bought Jaguar Land Rover for $2.3 billion in 2008 in another high-profile deal. Around the same time, the Aditya Birla Group-owned Hindalco Industries bought out the Atlanta-based Novelis Inc. for $6 billion.

Similarly, in the pharmaceuticals sector, Indian companies bought out foreign ones. Dr. Reddy's Laboratories, Aurobindo Pharma, Glenmark and Sun Pharma, all made significant acquisitions expanding their market presence in the US and Europe. India's prowess in pharmaceuticals is perhaps best illustrated by Cipla introducing a generic drug to treat HIV in 2001. Dr Yusuf K. Hamied, chairman of Cipla, battled global pharmaceutical giants to introduce HIV treatments that cost 30 times less than what global players were offering in African markets. The market was shaken by the introduction of these generics, and many companies were forced to lower their prices to compete. Cipla was soon supplying a third of all the HIV medications in Africa.[2] In the telecom sector, Airtel acquired Zain telecom in Africa in 2010 and gained access to 15 new markets in a deal worth $10.7 billion. This move was preceded by expansion into neighbouring countries such as Sri Lanka and Bangladesh.

It was not just big business houses that invested abroad during this time. Research shows that in the 1980s, 146 Indian firms invested abroad. In the 1990s, this number increased marginally

---

[2]'Breakthrough Briefs: India's Robin Hood of Drugs', United Nations Global Compact, 19 September 2016, https://bit.ly/3NTaLjI, accessed on 8 July 2022.

to approx. 250, jumped to approx. 1,000 in the early 2000s and to 1,800 plus by 2007.[3] The composition of outward FDI is similar to inward FDI. Gas and petroleum products, pharmaceuticals, chemicals, software development and ITeS accounted for a little more than half of all outward FDI between 1990 and 2007, the same study shows.

Another key aspect of this era of outward investments is that Indian companies, rather than going down the JV route, were creating subsidiaries in global markets. This again indicates our growing boldness and confidence in taking on global projects. Indian companies were also listing on global exchanges now. Infosys became the first company to list on the NASDAQ in March 1999. Since then, several Indian companies have gone on to list in global markets as well. HDFC Bank, ICICI Bank and MakeMyTrip are some such examples.

Flourish or Perish

These disruptions meant that new opportunities were created, but then incumbents would have to face a challenge. Domestic firms and their leaders had to adapt to this new reality and further develop their competitive advantages, as they would now be competing against not just foreign rivals but new domestic ones too.

A look at the equity markets will help us understand the evolution of the economy since the late 1980s/early 1990s. The BSE Sensex was formed in 1986 comprising 30 of the largest stocks trading on the BSE and quickly became a market benchmark. However, looking at the listed companies, and that too the top 30,

---

[3]Athukorala, Prema-Chandra, 'Outward Foreign Direct Investment from India', *Asian Development Review*, 26(2): 125–53, 2009; Kumar, Nagesh, 'Internationalization of Indian Enterprises: Patterns, Strategies, Ownership Advantages, and Implications', *Asian Economic Policy Review*, 3(2): 242–61, 2008.

perhaps does not give a complete picture of the transformation. Omkar Goswami has an interesting piece of analysis on the same.[4] Analysing corporate performance between 1991 and 2016, the author is able to distil the following: the top-line of companies grew at 10 per cent per annum, profits at 13 per cent and market capitalization at 19 per cent. The gross income of listed companies shot up from ₹2.6 lakh crore to ₹29 lakh crore, a tenfold increase. The changing nature of the economy is also evident from his analysis. Listed financial service companies grew in number from 34,000 to 12.8 lakh in these 25 years—a growth of 3,604 per cent! In contrast, the number of manufacturing companies grew by 626 per cent in 25 years, or 8 per cent per annum.

Of the 30 companies initially listed on the BSE Sensex, 27 were involved in manufacturing or mining, and none in banking, finance or technology.[5] Reliance Industries, ITC, Mahindra, Larsen & Toubro (L&T) are some names that figured then and continued to be on the index. The landscape is quite different today. Tech companies such as TCS, Infosys and Tech Mahindra are part of the index. Banks such as ICICI Bank, HDFC Bank, Kotak Mahindra Bank, IndusInd Bank and SBI are mainstays. Sun Pharma and Dr. Reddy's Laboratories are inclusions from the pharmaceutical sector. Notable inclusions especially in the energy sector are National Thermal Power Corporation, Oil and Natural Gas Corporation (ONGC) and Power Grid Corporation of India, which are under public ownership. Goswami notes that six of the top 10 companies by market capitalization in 2016,

[4]Goswami, Omkar, 'Changes and Challenges: Corporate India Since 1991', *India Transformed: 25 Years of Economic Reforms*, Rakesh Mohan (ed.), Penguin Random House India, New Delhi, 2017.
[5]Dhillon, Dilsher, 'The Story of Sensex Since Its Inception in 1986 Is the Story of India's Economy', *Business Insider India*, 3 April 2019, https://bit.ly/3ykYNJQ, accessed on 8 July 2022.

including TCS, Infosys, HDFC Bank and Sun Pharma, were either not listed or were non-existent in 1991.

Several companies established before the liberalization process were able to adapt to the changing reality and adjust their business models to thrive. The case of L&T is pertinent. Already a behemoth by the time of economic reforms, new opportunities and challenges arose. Being one of the few capital goods producers in India before the reforms meant that it would now be subject to fierce competition once the economy opened up. L&T responded by reducing costs to maintain competitiveness, while not sacrificing quality. In 1999, when Anil Naik took over as managing director and CEO, he set a target of making L&T a top global company.[6] Opportunities in the infrastructure sector were capitalized upon, especially in roads. Demerging parts of the business and retaining focus were other key elements of Naik's strategy to revitalize L&T.

ITC is another example of a company that has adapted to the changing times and continues to maintain its position in the markets. From being primarily focussed on its cigarette business, ITC has diversified, with revenues coming from sectors such as FMCG, hotels, paper, IT and agri-business. Back in 2000, ITC launched e-Choupal in Madhya Pradesh. Their focus on value-addition, exports and digitzation of agriculture is laudable. Due to their interventions at the farm level, farmers have been empowered through the efficient use of inputs and remunerative prices. Now, they are also foraying into millets, bringing value-added products to the consumer. They have also gone from strength-to-strength in the highly competitive FMCG segment with established domestic and global players. The synergies between their agri-business and FMCG business are paying off. Not only are shareholders benefitting

---

[6]Gopalakrishnan, R., and Pallavi Mody, *How Anil Naik Built L&T's Remarkable Growth Trajectory*, Rupa Publications, New Delhi, 2020.

but so are the lakhs of farmers connected to ITC from whom they procure wheat, potatoes and spices, among other products.

Under the leadership of Sanjiv Puri, ITC continues to be a key contributor to India's economy, redefining itself in the process. Puri has also contributed extensively to redefining India's agriculture sector as the Chairman of the High Level Expert Group on Agricultural Exports constituted by the Fifteenth Finance Commission. I had the pleasure of working with him closely while deliberating on a roadmap for digitally transforming India's agriculture sector. His keen understanding of the sector and vision stood out to me.

The Mahindra group, too, modernized and diversified its businesses. In 2002, it launched the Scorpio, which gave a new shape to India's sport utility vehicle (SUV) market. Today, the Group has a presence in 22 industries, ranging from agriculture, automobiles, defence manufacturing and finance to IT, among others.

Ratan Tata, a man who was ahead of his time and completely committed to nation-building, succeeded J.R.D. Tata as chairman of Tata Sons in the early 1990s. He set about expanding the businesses both domestically and globally. In fact, my brother, Ravi Kant, who was then the managing director of Tata Motors, played a key role in this turnaround and in the acquisition of Jaguar Land Rover by Tata Motors.

However, several prominent names such as Premier Auto and Hindustan Motors dropped out. Unable to cope with the additional competition first from Maruti Suzuki and then a spate of foreign players, these companies were no longer the behemoths they once were. Several manufacturing companies dropped out too. According to Goswami, these companies were unable to adapt to the competitive pressures that came with an open economy. The industries that were globally competitive thrived, such as those in services.

In manufacturing, many industries that benefitted from protection were inefficient compared to global benchmarks, and so was the quality of the products they were making. Gita Piramal cites the example of the Mafatlal Group, which was founded in 1905.[7] By the 1930s, the Group was thriving, with over nine cotton mills, along with interests in insurance, retail and shipping, among others. It had all the makings of a modern conglomerate. This trend continued in the 1960s, when it floated the National Organic Chemical Industries Limited (NOCIL) and entered the petrochemicals business well before anyone else in the private sector. However, by the 1990s, the cracks began to appear. As with other manufacturing firms of the time, technologically and operationally, its cotton mills were far behind the curve and uncompetitive in global markets. Similarly, NOCIL, while entering the petrochemicals industry before Reliance, was dwarfed in size compared to Reliance Industries Limited now.

Unchained Indians

Along with entrepreneurship, new career options also opened up which were not as popular before. Earlier, entering 'service' was considered a safe option for most of the youth. This could be in government services or professional services such as medicine, engineering or architecture, among others. Limited avenues for growth created limited avenues for employment. Post 1991, and particularly in the new millennium, new job designations and roles entered the lexicon, especially in the services sector. Jobs were being created in software, IT, ITeS, banking, tourism,

---

[7]Piramal, Gita, 'Animal Spirits: Stray Thoughts on the Nature of Entrepreneurship in India's Business Families After Liberalisation', *India Transformed: 25 Years of Economic Reforms*, Rakesh Mohan (ed.), Penguin Random House India, New Delhi, 2017.

hospitality, real estate, retail, civil aviation, FMCG, healthcare, education and several other fields. Lucrative opportunities in the private sector were now the preferred option of the best talent. Professional management of firms promoted a culture of meritocracy.

Incomes grew at such a pace that the youth entering the labour force were earning more than their parents were towards the end of their careers, writes Rama Bijapurkar.[8] This effect propelled the standard of living forward for millions of families. To see the effect, per capita incomes were about ₹31,000 in 1993–94, a couple of years after the reforms were initiated. Within 15 years, by 2007–08, per capita income (constant price) had crossed ₹60,000, growing at 4.5 per cent annually. In the 15 years before 1993–94, incomes had only grown at a rate of 2.2 per cent. Per capita consumption expenditure saw a 1.7 time increase during these times as well.

The explosion in wealth creation led to the rise of an increasingly dynamic middle class in India. Consumption expanded like never before. Take the example of cars. First was the issue of accessibility and affordability. Cars were simply out of the budgets of most families. Second, there was very little choice. A long waiting time was normal and would sometimes stretch for months. The same was the case with two-wheelers. Now, the Indian consumer could choose from several competing models in their budget, leverage finance and live their dream of one day owning a car.

Choices in consumer goods were limited. Televisions, while gaining popularity, were not as commonplace then. Air conditioners were rare. The FMCG industry saw more and more choices. Better-

---

[8]Bijapurkar, Rama, 'Consumer India's Journey from Zero to Hero', *India Transformed: 25 Years of Economic Reforms*, Rakesh Mohan (ed.), Penguin Random House India, New Delhi, 2017.

quality products were available at affordable prices. Black markets for consumer goods had developed in the pre-liberalization era, encouraging a parallel economy. Now, there was no such need for these black markets. However, this new middle class aspired for more than just the basic necessities. Foreign firms entered India and new brands were available. Domino's Pizza, McDonald's and Adidas opened their stores in 1996, and LG in 1997. The traditional markets in towns saw swanky new showrooms of foreign brands. Indian brands were forced to compete, perish or be bought out. This happened in the case of Thums Up, a popular Indian cola brand bought out by Coca-Cola.

Many have tended to question this story of India's middle class, including *The Economist* magazine in 2018.[9] However, as we—my colleagues (Vaibhav Kapoor and Ranveer Nagaich) and I—wrote, the estimates put out by *The Economist* vastly underestimated the size of India's middle class. The magazine asserted that India's middle class was no larger than 78 million people. However, our analysis showed that in making such estimates, purchasing power parity must be considered. For instance, the threshold of income used to define the middle class was in far excess of the globally defined poverty lines.[10] Taking more realistic benchmarks, our analysis showed that the size of India's middle class had swelled to 304.2 million people by 2004–05. In the next seven years, by 2011–12, this size had effectively doubled to 604.3 million. However, there is some stratification within the middle class in India. Even if we exclude the lower-middle class from consideration, the size of India's middle class still comes to 158 million, close to double than that projected by *The Economist*.

[9]"India Has a Hole Where Its Middle Class Should Be', *The Economist*, 13 January 2018, https://econ.st/3yt0c0W, accessed on 8 July 2022.
[10]Kant, Amitabh, et al., 'India's Burgeoning Middle-Class', *Mint*, 23 January 2018, https://bit.ly/2RAXhwQ, accessed on 8 July 2022.

The media industry too has grown by leaps and bounds since liberalization. Televisions themselves only started to gain popularity during the 1983 Cricket World Cup. Programming, however, was limited. Many readers may recall the monopoly Doordarshan enjoyed in television programming prior to the 1990s. As part of the reforms package, private and foreign broadcasters were allowed to operate in India. Both Indian and foreign companies jumped at the chance. Zee TV became the first private channel in India. Sun TV was launched in 1993. Star India started programming international content through its entertainment and movie channels such as Star TV and Star Movies. Sony Entertainment Television (SET) was launched in 1995. The next decade saw international giants such CNN enter India.

India's media landscape was transformed like never before. Consumers now had dozens of channels to choose from, rather than a handful. This also had a knock-on effect of changing attitudes and perceptions of the Indian consumer. Not only was international programming widely available in India but localized content creation received a fillip too. The advent of the 24-hour news cycle saw dedicated news channels launched, again led by private enterprise. NDTV, Aaj Tak and CNBC saw their advent during this era.

At the same time, we also see a rise in the advertising industry in India. Of course, the industry existed even before liberalization and had given iconic advertisements, but the profusion in television channels created even more avenues and competition. The rising trend of consumerism and middle class provided a huge target audience. The Indian consumer was increasingly connected. From the days when one had to pay handsomely for cellular phones and associated services, costs had fallen to among the cheapest in the world. Internet access had improved, especially in middle-class homes, and the Indian consumer was now connected globally.

A Sleeping Elephant Rises

The globally connected Indian also became a globe-trotting Indian. The entry of the private sector, along with an increase in incomes across the board, greatly democratized air travel in India. While air travel has seen considerable churn, the IndiGo story stands out. In 2005, capitalizing on the low-cost carrier phenomenon, Rahul Bhatia co-founded India's first true low-cost airline. The next year, they launched operations, with a flight going from New Delhi to Guwahati. Within six years, they were among the largest airlines in India. Despite starting small, they did not lack ambition. An intricate understanding of the industry and a keen eye on the future enabled the airline to fly high. As Shelley Vishwajeet recounts, IndiGo made global headlines for placing an order for 100 Airbus A320 aircrafts in 2005.[11] The deal, worth $6.5 billion, stunned competitors and industry analysts alike. This large order also ensured that at a time when competitors were struggling to add capacity, IndiGo had a pipeline of aircraft incoming. The structure of the deals meant that IndiGo was able to secure discounts on the list price and put in place a 'sale-and-leaseback' agreement. Moreover, Airbus or the engine supplier would be responsible for engine repair. This lowered their operating costs and presented a cleaner balance sheet than their competitors, notes Vishwajeet.

The space entered by IndiGo was highly competitive. SpiceJet commenced operations in 2005 like GoAir, which was promoted by the Wadia Group. Air Deccan commanded a substantial market share at the time as well. However, IndiGo turned into India's leading airline because of the key pillars of its strategy that set them apart: on time performance, low-cost connectivity and high

[11]Vishwajeet, Shelley, *The IndiGo Story: Inside the Upstart That Redefined Indian Aviation*, Rupa Publications, New Delhi, 2018.

standards of service. It is for these reasons that I have admired Bhatia. Personally, I have always preferred to fly IndiGo, despite being entitled to full-service airlines. Rarely have I found an Indigo flight delayed. I only hope that they continue to maintain these high standards and continue to grow and expand not merely in domestic but also international markets. This will enable India to position its airports as global hubs of trade and tourism.

Multiple daily flights connected India's centres of technology, commerce, industry and finance. This also had the knock-on effect of making railways improve their services, as long-route travel by air was increasingly affordable and accessible.

However, it was not air and rail travel alone that triggered a take-off of Indian tourism. It was buttressed by a campaign that took the world by storm—Incredible India. It was launched in 2002 when travel to India was down in the dumps—in the wake of the destruction of the World Trade Center, the resultant war on Afghanistan and the attack on the Indian parliament in 2001. Driven in partnership with the private sector, support sectors such as aviation, hotels and infrastructure grew in tandem, and new areas such as rural medical value and ecological tourism developed.

The genesis of the 'Incredible India' campaign can be actually traced to my role as secretary (Tourism) in the government of Kerala, in which I was fortunate to drive the state's incredible journey from being an unknown destination to India's number-one tourism hotspot on the back of the 'God's Own Country' campaign. However, this turnaround was not without its challenges. Prior to being posted as tourism secretary, I was without a posting for a very long time. The tourism posting was a punishment posting for me. In those days, no one travelled to Kerala. Rajasthan and Kashmir were the preferred destinations for tourists. The only tourist destination in Kerela was Kovalam, which had emerged as a low-value, charter destination for travellers from the UK. The groups used to be full of cobblers and garbage collectors, as rates were as low as $20 a night. But since the development of the beach was unplanned and unsustainable, Kovalam was a disaster. The beautiful beach was now filled with garbage and filth. In fact, one of my first tasks in my new role was the clean-up of the Kovalam beach.

We then began to develop new products to draw tourists to the backwaters of Kerala. We promoted local craftsmanship to build houseboats in which not a single nail is used; the entire boat was held together by knots. Unlike the Kashmiri houseboats, the ones in Kerala are constantly moving, allowing one to get a glimpse of the rural life of Kerala. Tourists get to engage with the community and indulge in activities like catching their own fish. We realized that a lot of the carpenters had gone away to the Gulf; we had a tough time bringing them back. Owing to our sustained efforts, houseboats have now evolved as sustainable products. They use solar energy and chemical toilet treatments. We also promoted Ayurveda as a tourism and wellness product. As a result, people came and stayed in Kerala for long periods of time.

At that time, Kerala was known for trade militancy, which ended up destroying jobs and killing industries. We engaged TCS for the creation of tourism satellite accounts. These demonstrated that tourism was creating a large number of jobs, particularly for women, leading to tourism getting widely accepted across the political spectrum. Another key aspect of our success was that we did not develop Kerala Tourism as a government product. While the government focussed on branding, marketing and connectivity, the experiences were created by the private sector. Unique top-class resorts came up, serving high-value tourists.

Thus, Kerala's positioning was not that of a mass-market tourist destination but rather as a high-value, upmarket one. Branding was crucial to the success of the 'God's Own Country' campaign. Working with an agency like Stark Communications was a unique experience. Some of the finest creative minds worked on this campaign, bringing in fresh energy and vitality. Their creativity played a key role. We managed to keep Kerala's appeal fresh by innovating new products and through branding. Kerala, for the first time, demonstrated that branding mattered.

In more ways than one, Kerala takes credit for being the first state in India to comprehend the significance and importance of tourism as a catalyst for growth and a job creator. Its worldwide success as a tourism destination represents triumph of PPP. Kerala's focus on its rich tapestry of traditional products—backwaters, houseboats, cuisine, the traditional martial art Kalaripayattu and the traditional dance forms of Koodiyattam, Theyyam and Mohiniyattam—differentiated it from any other destination of the world. The state's private sector never aped the West. It created its own unique flavour. The turning point came when the *National Geographic Traveler*, after extensive research, termed it 'one of the ten exotic paradises of the world'. Kerala evolved as a high-value, upmarket destination. Its private entrepreneurs have been the critical force in implementing innovative initiatives, in building a sustainable and tourist-friendly destination and preserving the culture and tradition of the land.

While I was secretary (Tourism), I received a call from Brajesh Mishra, principal secretary to PM Atal Bihari Vajpayee. He informed me that the PM would like to holiday in Kerala. It would be my job to plan an itinerary where the PM would be left alone and not surrounded by politicians and bureaucrats. I made all the arrangements for his stay at the Taj.

We hosted the PM for a week. On one of the days, we accompanied him to the backwaters on a houseboat, giving him a feel of the area. That evening, Ashok Saikia, the then joint secretary in the Prime Minister's Office, suggested to the PM that I should be brought to Delhi to drive India tourism. PM Vajpayee then enquired as to whether I had applied for a tenure in the GoI. When I replied that I had not yet, the PM laughed and said that I shouldn't apply because if I did, Saikia would end up posting me in the women and child development department rather than tourism. We all laughed at that and it seemed to be the end of the story.

I applied for tenure in the GoI 15 months later, and the Civil Services Board selected me to go to the Ministry of Finance. Around the same time, I got a call from Saikia, asking if I had applied to GoI. I said yes. He recalled the discussion we had had about moving to the Ministry of Tourism. I responded that there were no posts for my level at the ministry. Saikia responded that it was none of my business whether a post existed or not. Soon enough, a vacancy was created in the Ministry of Tourism when the then incumbent was transferred to the Ministry of Labour and Employment. That is how I ended up as joint secretary in the Ministry of Tourism.

Within a few weeks of joining, I realized that India was often referred to as a 'sleeping giant' or 'sleeping elephant' in the global tourism industry. Even though the country's many assets had been eulogized at every international trade platform, and its prospects and potential were deliberated at every global tourism meet, yet India's performance was far from laudable. For more than a decade, till 2002, India's share of the world tourism traffic had remained static at about 0.38 per cent. The chasm between potential and performance was widened as a result of various factors, the worst being the perception that tourism was an elitist activity set in the background of five-star hotels, recreation and pleasure. Somehow, the actual benefits of tourism—its multiplier effect on employment, infrastructure and community growth—all seemed to have been miserably lost.

As soon as I joined, the 9/11 attacks happened in New York. There was war in Afghanistan and our Parliament was attacked in December 2001. Many countries issued travel advisories against travelling to India. Our hotel occupancy rates plummeted. This was also the time when Malaysia, Singapore and Australia stopped their advertising campaigns. We approached leading tour operators abroad. All of them said the same thing: that there was no demand for travel to India.

At the peak of the crisis, we launched the 'Incredible India' campaign, which was more than mere advertising. The brand-building process was driven in partnership with the private sector and comprised building relationship with international tour operators and travel writers, and aggressive marketing on electronic and social media. The Experience India Society comprising leading hoteliers and tour operators brought in an element of fresh creativity to the campaign. The thrust for PPP in tourism was provided by leading hoteliers. They had the vision to raise private-sector resources to complement government outlays for destination marketing of India.

Building up India's tourism brand was a collaborative effort. The contributions of the Indian Hotels Company Ltd (IHCL) in building India's tourism brand stands out. Jamsetji Tata's vision of a luxury hotel was realized in 1903 with the iconic Taj Mahal Palace Hotel. Since then, IHCL has almost been synonymous with India's tourism. With the restoration of the Lake Palace into a luxury hotel in 1971, IHCL, through its Taj brand, has led the conversion of old royal palaces into luxury hotels with modern amenities. Taj Falaknuma Palace in Hyderabad and Taj Rambagh Palace in Jaipur are other prominent examples. The brand was among the first to open a luxury resort in Goa, and then in Kerala, while I was the tourism secretary.

IHCL was quick to build up a portfolio of business hotels with strategic foresight. Now, under the leadership of Puneet Chhatwal, MD and CEO, they are set to continue their remarkable standards while being the ambassadors for India's brand of hospitality. Continuing with their legacy of firsts, they have been the first to set up unique, world class resorts in the Andamans and Coorg. They are also in the process of setting up two greenfield resort projects in Lakshadweep. Sustainability will be a key element of these operations, continuing their rich legacy of responsibility towards the local communities and environment. These destinations can provide serious competition to beach resort destinations in the vicinity.

I must make a special mention of the role played by employees of the Taj Mahal Palace hotel during the 26/11 terror attacks in Mumbai. The actions of the Taj employees saved the lives of many that night, with several employees losing their lives while protecting the guests. This dedication and bravery of the employees towards keeping their guests safe is inspiring. According to a case study at Harvard University, during this terror attack, Taj employees gave customer service a whole new meaning. And I wholeheartedly agree. Deshpande and Raina attribute this response to the organizational values of Taj Hotels.[12] Their recruitment strategy, training and mentoring, and rewards system have been cited as key factors. There are many lessons for us to take away from this incident—the employees' dedication to their values, being among the most important.

Another group that has become synonymous with India's tourism industry is the Oberoi Group. India's first modern, luxury 5-star hotel, the Oberoi Intercontinental (Icon), was opened in Delhi in

---

[12]Deshpande, Rohit, and Anjali Raina. 'The Ordinary Heroes of the Taj', *Harvard Business Review*, Vol. 89, No. 12, pp. 119–123, 2011, https://bit.ly/42J3Nq6. Accessed on 28 March 2023.

1965. The Oberoi Group and PRS Oberoi, in particular, must be credited with establishing a brand of luxury through their 'vilas' brand, which includes iconic properties such as Udaivilas in Udaipur, Rajvilas in Jaipur and Amarvilas in Agra, among others.

These brands are not limited to India. They have also gone global. Heritage properties in destinations such as The Pierre in New York and St. James' Court in London were acquired by Taj Hotels. The Oberoi Group restored properties such as The Windsor in Melbourne, Australia, and Mena House in Cairo, Egypt. These brands have established a legacy of customer-centricity and played a key role in building India's tourism brand. While the demand for luxury destinations was growing, increased trade and commerce also necessitated the rise of business hotels.

As Indian tourism worked with some of the finest creative minds in the advertising world, including V. Sunil and Ogilvy & Mather, to create a strong destination image, the brand had to be constantly kept alive and fresh. Every year, a new creative campaign was unveiled in the global market. The objective was to create an impact on the consumers in a focussed and targeted manner. A marketing-led strategy resulted in a rise in demand which, in turn, led to the emergence of new airlines and the development of new airports at Mumbai, Delhi, Hyderabad and Bangalore under PPP.

Incredible India was defined by creativity, brilliant execution and constant innovation, which became the hallmarks of the campaign. During this campaign, I realized the importance of not working on the principle of lowest cost. I always believed that good creativity necessitates paying well, and therefore, the quality-cum-cost principle is much better than just the lowest cost, which leads to shoddy quality at high costs. Further, it is important for officers to do things in a transparent manner and learn to work with the best in the field.

Growth Story Under Threat

The economy grew at a steady pace till 2008 when the global financial crisis hit followed by the Great Recession. India's response included a combined monetary and fiscal stimulus, which kept growth rates elevated during the worst years of the crisis. However, it has been debated whether the fiscal policies followed during this time ended up harming the competitiveness of the economy in the medium term. In *Backstage*, Ahluwalia notes that the third fiscal stimulus, announced before the elections of 2009, could have been oriented towards public expenditure on infrastructure.[13] However, tax concessions and expanded social sector expenditure led to a ballooning fiscal deficit and inflation.[14] We saw how growth rates declined in the years 2011–12, 2012–13 and 2013–14, by whatever base of GDP we have. The economy had clearly overheated by this time, and this is reflected in the double-digit inflation. No doubt, oil prices had shot up considerably, but excessive domestic demand too led to an inflation spike. Investments in infrastructure were perhaps the need of the hour, rather than tax cuts.

Domestic factors also contributed to the downturn in economic performance. While the economy was riding high, the reform by gradualism agenda eventually stalled. Though important social sector schemes such as the Mahatma Gandhi National Rural Employment Guarantee Act, Right to Education and National Food Security Act were launched during this time, there were also legislations passed that hampered economic growth. The Right to Fair Compensation and Transparency in Land Acquisition, Rehabilitation and Resettlement (LARR) Act, 2013, is a case in

---

[13]Singh Ahluwalia, Montek, *Backstage: The Story behind India's High Growth Years,* Rupa Publications, 2020.
[14]Mehra, Puja, *The Lost Decade 2008–18: How India's Growth Story Devolved into Growth Without a Story,* Penguin eBury Press, 2019.

point. N.C. Saxena, former member of the Planning Commission and National Advisory Council, had been highly critical of the LARR Act, terming it both 'anti-industry' and 'anti-farmer'.[15] He noted that the increased compensation would hardly be a concern for industry, but the level of red-tapism created would. Acquiring one acre of land would take up to three years and would have to pass through a multitude of approvals. This is because the LARR Act created several committees comprising activists and experts and each would have to approve the acquisition. Illustrating further, Social Impact Assessment would be carried out by a committee, which would then be vetted by an expert group. There would also be a rehabilitation and resettlement (R&R) committee, apart from state-level committees and national monitoring committee, explains Saxena. The multiple committees and approvals meant that even if someone wanted to acquire land and was ready to pay all the prescribed compensation, it would still take them years to acquire the land. This delay would mean that the compensation paid to farmers, for instance, would also be delayed. So, this Act was unable to deliver on protecting farmers' rights and also added layers of bureaucracy to the land acquisition process, making it ripe for rent-seeking behaviour.

At the same time, fuelled by easy fiscal and monetary policies, there was a debt problem developing in the economy. Corporates had borrowed large sums of money and expanded capex considerably. However, funding long-term assets through short-term debt was a problem that did not merit consideration in an era of low interest rates and ample liquidity. Once the financial crisis hit and the RBI started raising interest rates, the cost of borrowing stressed the balance sheets of corporates. Slowing demand in the economy as the fiscal stimulus ran out,

---

[15]Saxena, N.C., 'The Land Bill Is Pro-Bureaucracy, Anti-Farmer', *Business Standard*, 2 September 2013, https://bit.ly/3ynERG9, accessed on 8 July 2022.

led to deceleration of growth. The twin balance sheet problem the economy faced for several years started to come to the fore.

Non-performing assets (NPAs) started to mount. The genesis of this problem actually lay in the boom years of the economy that saw confidence in the growth story at all-time highs. However, an element of irrational exuberance crept in, as per many.[16] Large loans were made towards infrastructure projects such as in power, steel and real estate. The *Economic Survey 2016–17* notes that between 2004 and 2009, non-food bank credit effectively doubled.[17] Thus, a large part of India's rising investment rates, particularly corporate, were financed through debt. At the same time, banks played a dominant role in the economy as the primary issuers of credit. Corporate bond markets were relatively nascent. So, a bulk of the financing needs of industry, which requires long-term credit for long-term projects, was met by banks. In the aftermath of the global financial crisis and the Great Recession, expansionary fiscal and monetary policy insulated India from any immediate impacts.

However, during the turn of the decade, inflation started to rise, raising the cost of these projects significantly. The global commodity boom saw prices of inputs and intermediate goods soar. Therefore, the projects ended up costing more than originally envisioned. Even though the Licence Raj had been dismantled, a web of procedures, approvals and regulations were still dominant. For large projects, land acquisition and environmental clearances, combined with procedural delays, meant that projects were often delayed, further adding to the costs. During this period

---

[16]'Raghuram Rajan Explains the Origins of India's NPA Crisis', *The Wire*, 12 September 2018, https://bit.ly/3yMTmVw, accessed on 8 July 2022.

[17]*Economic Survey 2016–17*, Government of India, Ministry of Finance, Department of Economic Affairs Economic Division, January 2017, p. 86, https://bit.ly/2s5AXQ0, accessed on 8 July 2022.

of financial upheaval, forex outflows meant that the rupee had depreciated considerably. Firms that had borrowed abroad saw costs of borrowings increase. So did domestic firms, as the RBI had increased interest rates, as expansionary monetary policy was wound down after inflation spiked. Large projects saw delays and increased costs, both in terms of interest and raw materials. Finally, the effects of the Great Recession and the fizzling out of the fiscal stimulus meant that growth lost steam as well. The revenues of these projects were made on the basis of the economy continuing on the high-growth path seen earlier. So, with rising costs and lower-than-expected revenues, it is no surprise that these projects accumulated losses and were unable to meet their debt obligations.

The scale of the problem can be seen through the interest coverage ratio. A ratio of above 1 implies that earnings are enough to cover interest payments on debt. A ratio of less than 1 implies that the firm did not earn even enough to cover interest payments. According to the *Economic Survey 2016–17*, nearly 40 per cent of corporate debt was owed by companies with an interest coverage ratio of less than 1, mostly in the power and metals sector. On the other hand, most of this corporate debt was concentrated in PSBs, rather than private-sector banks. This further crippled the growth of credit in the economy.

There are several explanations that have been put forward that explain why a bulk of NPAs had become concentrated in PSBs. A lack of due diligence, combined with irrational exuberance, is one. Eager to capitalize on the economic boom, lending expanded considerably, without due regard to the financial viability of the projects. Second, the process of 'evergreening' loans, essentially granting new loans to cover the old ones, kept the brewing problem under wraps. The survey notes that these loans were initially restructured in the hope that demand would pick up and these projects would soon turn viable. As much as 20 per cent of all loans, including these evergreened and restructured loans issued by PSBs, were NPAs. These governance issues of PSBs were perhaps a key contributing factor.

The Asset Quality Review (AQR) initiated by the RBI in 2015 revealed the scale of the problem. This twin balance sheet problem had wide-ranging ramifications for the economy and private enterprise. Credit growth to industry, especially small industries, slowed considerably. Bank managers, especially in PSBs, in fear of increased scrutiny in case the investments went south, were increasingly conservative. This strangling of credit meant that many productive investments were not funded.

This episode is also reflective of India's business environment then. Sadly, while the economy had been liberalized considerably, ease of doing business was hardly at the top of the agenda. Our rank of 142 in the 2014 World Bank's Ease of Doing Business (EoDB) rankings reflected this.

Macroeconomic pressures began to break through the papered over cracks. The now infamous 'Taper Tantrum' of 2013 showed that India's macroeconomic position was perhaps more fragile than believed. As the US Federal Reserve announced a reduction in quantitative easing policies, capital flowed out from developing markets to developed ones, and India was no exception. Between May and August 2013, the rupee depreciated by nearly 20 per cent.[18] The fiscal deficit remained elevated, while growth was slowing.

Progress effectively stagnated. The expansion in public expenditure, especially revenue expenditure at the expense of capital expenditure, brought the need for fiscal consolidation. This meant that at a time when public expenditure should have been

---

[18]Tewari, Maulik, 'All You Wanted to Know About Taper Tantrum', *The Hindu BusinessLine*, 1 March 2021, https://bit.ly/3O6gHWN, accessed on 8 July 2022.

oriented to building infrastructure and unlocking bottlenecks, it stagnated, further shackling growth. Domestic private investment was also subdued owing to a variety of factors.

At this point, the reform agenda needed to go further. Several sectors and areas were left out of this agenda, preferring to take a gradual approach. However, gradualism soon had given way to inaction. Many reasons are cited for this. First, political compulsions may have stalled the reform agenda as even within the serving United Progressive Alliance-II government, there was little agreement on economic policies. Take the example of the India–US nuclear deal, where support for the central government was withdrawn by the left parties in 2008. Second, a string of scandals relating to coal allocations, 2G spectrum allocations and corruption in the Commonwealth Games severely hampered India's image in global markets of being the next big growth story. Around the same time, decisions regarding retrospective taxation further hampered India's image as a viable destination for foreign investment.

Decision-making and policymaking were practically frozen, with inflation galloping. In fact, this phase, often described as one of 'policy paralysis', was characterized by a situation in which no decision was preferred to any decision.

The incomplete reforms of the 1990s were now a bottleneck to India's growth and prosperity. While important social sector schemes were launched, they ended up harming the fiscal health of the nation. Public investments in infrastructure suffered as a result. The need of the hour was to usher in a new paradigm of growth and development, something we have seen unfold since 2014.

FIVE

A NEW PARADIGM:
REVITALIZING THE ECONOMY

The mood of the nation saw a shift when a new government, headed by PM Narendra Modi, was overwhelmingly elected in 2014. This ushered in a new paradigm. The PM must be given credit for the paradigm shift he has brought about not just in processes, but also for his focus on ease of doing business, ease of living for the common citizen and for eliminating rules, regulations, procedures and a vast number of outdated laws.

I have been fortunate to have played a role in this change through my work first as secretary, Department of Industrial Policy and Promotion (DIPP) and later as CEO, NITI Aayog. Prime Minister Modi played an instrumental role in my appointment as the CEO. When I was retiring as Secretary, DIPP, I had applied for the post of the Chairman of the Competition Commission of India (CCI). I was shortlisted for the role, and the file was approved by everyone, except the PM. As it happened, I called upon the PM for some other work, and asked for his blessings for my post as Chairman, CCI. The PM remarked that I would have his blessings, but not for this post. He said that I should continue to work in government, and that I was not cut out for the role of Chairman, CCI. Soon, thereafter, I was posted as CEO, NITI Aayog. Initially, I was disappointed. It was a newly created body, with none of the power, authority or resources of the body it replaced, the Planning Commission. There were many challenges we had to overcome.

Looking back, these were some of the best years of my career. This is perhaps one of the few times when government work has been carried out with so much zeal and enthusiasm. However, this was not just limited to certain departments or ministries. The whole of the government was galvanized and pressed into action. A strong monitoring and evaluation mechanism was developed, leveraging technology. Through PRAGATI—the information and communication technology-based, multimodal platform for proactive governance and timely implementation—for instance, infrastructure projects and public grievances are monitored at the level of the PM himself. I have been part of several infrastructure review meetings chaired by the PM in which projects and their bottlenecks are resolved and policy decisions taken.

The change has not just been effected at a micro level. The big picture has not been lost in this quest. Economic reforms have taken centre stage since then. Reforms that have been on the anvil for decades have been carried out. Efforts have been centred around formalizing the economy, a renewed thrust on manufacturing and exports, and development of world-class infrastructure. It was also recognized that simple economic reforms would not be enough. Governance reforms were needed across all levels of government, especially in making India an easier place to do business in. But perhaps, most crucially, it has been recognized that private-sector leadership would be crucial to India achieving its development ambitions. Formalizing the economy would be the crucial first step.

Formalizing the Economy

The reform agenda since 2014 takes forward and builds momentum on the reform agenda of the 1990s and early 2000s. One of the first major big-ticket reforms initiated within the first few years of the National Democratic Alliance government was the introduction of the Insolvency and Bankruptcy Code (IBC) in 2016. Not only was starting a business in India a mammoth task, but shutting one down was perhaps an even bigger one. In a dynamic business environment, both operations should be easy. The lack of a modern law on bankruptcy had several implications for the economy and private enterprise. First, it discouraged entrepreneurship and risk-taking. The hurdles one had to jump through to close a business meant that entrepreneurs often wasted precious time wrapped up in bureaucracy and paperwork to close their old ventures rather than spending time on developing new ones. Second, bankruptcy proceedings took an inordinate amount of time, thus hampering the credit markets as well. Debtors were often unable to liquidate firms in a timely manner, stacking up their losses as well.

The introduction of the IBC brought the much-needed clarity in bankruptcy law. Shashwat Alok, Aditya Kuvalekar, Rajeev Mantri and Prasanna Tantri revealed the benefits of the IBC.[1] First, studying the fraction of cases resolved within a specific time frame, the authors found that the IBC took significantly less time to resolve cases than the erstwhile Board for Industrial and Financial Reconstruction (BIFR). A large number of erstwhile BIFR cases were also subsumed and resolved by the IBC. They conclude that the IBC has significantly outperformed the BIFR when it comes to the speed of resolving cases. They further emphasize that apart from the speed of resolution, IBC functions as an effective disciplining tool, discouraging the behaviour that devastated the health of India's banking sector.

The introduction of GST in 2017 has been considered by many as independent India's most landmark tax reform. Prior to the GST, a litany of indirect taxes existed, each requiring separate registration and filing norms. The cascading effect of taxes increased costs as well. This added to the cost of doing business and encouraged firms to remain in the informal and unorganized sector. Indirect taxes varied across states and hampered interstate movement of goods, further harming the competitiveness of manufactured goods. Long lines of trucks at state borders caused huge bottlenecks.

---

[1] Alok, Shashwat, et al., 'Effective and Efficient: The Insolvency and Bankruptcy Code', *The Indian Express*, 22 April 2022, https://bit.ly/3bZ9ESn, accessed on 8 July 2022.

With the introduction of the GST, central VAT and state VAT, Central Sales Tax and service tax are just a few of the taxes subsumed under the GST. Now, indirect taxes on most goods were the same across the nation, making it an integrated market. According to the *Economic Survey 2017–18*, a 50 per cent increase in unique indirect taxpayers was seen.[2] Taxes became easier to file, with invoices automatically matched for input tax credit (ITC). The provision of ITC has perhaps been the biggest factor in the increased formalization seen in the economy. This not only removed the cascading effect of taxes, but firms could offset taxes due through ITC. Long lines of trucks at interstate borders and barriers to internal trade were now a thing of the past.

The evolution of the GST is a testament to the fact that the Centre and states can work together to design the country's biggest tax reform. For example, the formation of the GST Council heralds a new era of Centre–state relations. With representation from all states and union territories, the GST Council is the first such Centre–state body with full decision-making powers impacting the fiscal health of the nation. Decisions taken by the Council are based on voting, with states carrying two-thirds of the vote share and the Centre, one-third. During and after the roll-out of the GST, every decision has been taken by consensus, reflecting the true spirit of cooperative federalism.

Of course, implementing such a system was a Herculean task, and the system continues to evolve. Now, revenue streams from GST seem to be stabilizing. In the seven months since April 2022, GST revenues have been above the ₹1.4 lakh crore mark. November 2022 GST collection stood at ₹1.46 lakh crore, up by 11 per cent year-on-year. The economic recovery, together with

---

[2]'GST data reveals 50% increase in number of Indirect Taxpayers', Press Information Bureau, Government of India, Ministry of Finance, 29 January 2018, https://bit.ly/3RzNeXH, accessed on 10 September 2022.

strong anti-evasive action, has led to the rise in GST collections. As the economy continues to grow and recover, GST revenues will be a robust source of financing development expenditure.

A knock-on effect of GST is that now, vast amounts of data, millions of invoices and e-way bills are being generated by the GST network. With tools such as data analytics, artificial intelligence (AI) and machine learning (ML), this data can be a source of increasing credit penetration, through devising cash flow-based lending models.

Real estate was one sector that floundered in the aftermath of the global financial crisis and Great Recession. As the economy slowed down in 2012–13, this sector felt the full brunt of the funding crunch. Coinciding with a boom in global commodity prices, rising interest costs and subdued demand meant that many projects were soon unviable, like they were in the power sector. This again had a multiplier impact on the economy. Debt-saddled firms were unable to raise further revenues to restart or complete projects. Banks, saddled with this debt, were unable to raise lending to other productive sectors. Construction employment, which is a huge employer of labour, especially of that exiting agriculture, saw a decline as well. This saw domestic consumption and savings rates remain subdued. Homeowners, having committed substantial financial resources, found themselves 'owning' incomplete projects, with no date for possession of their asset in sight. This created a negative risk perception around this sector, which hampered demand.

The need of the hour was to create an environment where the rights of both developers and buyers were protected. A robust real estate market would have manifold benefits for the Indian economy. This was achieved through the introduction of the Real Estate Regulatory Authority (RERA) in all states. It not only protected the rights of homebuyers but also promoted the development of private enterprise by maintaining their solvency and creditworthiness. For instance, the creation of an escrow account for construction purposes meant that funds could not be diverted and could only be used to fund projects. The clause allowing for extension in completion of projects also promoted the long-term health of the sector, as witnessed during Covid-19. Many projects were stalled owing to lockdowns and a lack of workers or other supply-side issues. Had these provisions not existed in the Act, there would have been no way for these project deadlines to be extended, which would have severely impacted the health of this sector. Again, this encouraged developers and agents to on-board themselves on the RERA system, promoting voluntary compliance.

Direct taxes is another area that has seen considerable change. The system that existed post-Independence saw a narrow tax base develop. High marginal personal income tax rates had encouraged under-reporting of income, aiding the parallel or 'black' economy. High corporate tax rates relative to other countries added to the uncompetitive nature of our manufacturing sector. The year 2017 saw a lowered personal income tax rate, and in 2019, corporate taxes were reduced to 22 per cent, making the effective rate (including cess, etc.) equivalent to 25 per cent, at par with most nations in our neighbourhood. In 2020, the year most impacted by the pandemic, the government unveiled a comprehensive reform agenda that included a new, voluntary personal income tax regime. The introduction of the Taxpayers' Charter, efforts to reduce litigation and the use of technology have moved the system away from one of enforcement to facilitation. Most new schemes and rates have been made voluntary, allowing individuals and corporates to choose the regime that best suits them. Voluntary compliance, as in the case of GST, has broadened the tax base.

A lot of credit for formalizing the economy must be given

to the then Finance Minister, (late) Arun Jaitley. He ensured that the GST was rolled out with the consensus of all states, with not a single issue going to vote. His efforts to bring in the IBC finally gave India a formal bankruptcy law. I first met him when he was President of the Delhi University Students Union in the '70s. I had just enrolled in St. Stephen's College and met him for an interview for an episode of 'Roving Microphone', run by All India Radio. His razor-sharp intellect left me deeply impressed. Later, while I was Secretary (DIPP), we interacted on numerous occasions while working on ease of doing business, liberalizing the FDI regime and the IBC. His legal acumen and clarity of thought always shone through. Despite his serious illness, he was gracious enough to launch a book I had edited. He delivered a brilliant lecture, despite his doctors advising him not to speak. My regret is that I never got to work directly with him.

Renewed Thrust on Competitiveness

One glaring gap in India's development story so far was the relative lack of expansion in the manufacturing and exports sectors. The share of manufacturing in India's GDP stayed more or less constant in the 25 years since the reforms. Exports growth was driven primarily by service exports and India continued to run current account deficits. The growth experience of other Asian countries had shown the importance of a robust manufacturing and exports sector.

It was recognized early on in the tenure of this government that manufacturing and exports would play a crucial role in scripting India's development story. This was first elucidated through the 'Make in India' campaign, which I had the good fortune of driving. Initially, the logo we selected was that of an elephant, expertly put together by V. Sunil, our design partner. We made three presentations to the PM on the logo and branding of Make in India. After several rounds of discussion with the PM, it was changed into a lion, derived from the Ashoka Chakra.

With the logo finalized, we started with three key objectives. The first was promoting ease of doing business. We realized that Indian businesses and entrepreneurs still had to deal with a litany of regulations, permissions, forms and clearances before they could commence operations. Often, these clearances and permissions stalled projects, making them financially unviable, even before they were formally commissioned. If we were to compete with other nations in export markets, then the costs of doing business in India would have to be brought down significantly. And that is exactly what happened.

I recall my first presentation to PM Modi on Ease of Doing Business as secretary (DIPP). At the time, India was ranked a dismal 142 in the rankings published by the World Bank. Though this was my initial presentation in New Delhi, I had, in my capacity as CEO of the Delhi Mumbai Industrial Corridor, interacted with Mr Modi several times while he was the chief minister (CM) of Gujarat. At that time, he had identified Dholera for development as an industrial city. Even back then, I was impressed by his vision and his ability to see the big picture. I had visited Gujarat several times as a speaker at the Vibrant Gujarat Summit, so I had a working relationship with him before he became the PM.

Since then, I have had the good fortune of working with the PM on numerous initiatives, such as Make in India, Startup India, PLIs, Aspirational Districts, eMobility, Green hydrogen and Covid-19 management. He always brings a fresh dimension, is a techie at heart, has immense clarity of mind and is very grassroots oriented.

I think I would have made the most number of presentations since he took office in 2014 beginning with as secretary (DIPP).

During the course of the first presentation, PM Modi directed us to focus on ease of doing business. He made it absolutely clear that the job of the government is to have predictable and consistent policies and to make things easy and simple for the private sector.

His experience as a CM really came to the fore during the meeting. It was the first time I found a PM talking about scrapping rules, regulations and acts. He spoke not about making new laws but doing away with the old ones. The PM was clear in his view that India had to become an easier place to do business in. The web of rules and regulations was choking India's private enterprise and the entire focus needed to shift towards its promotion and facilitation. This reflected the new attitude with which we had to work.

We set about our task in earnest. We identified the key areas for improvement and started taking corrective action. Automating processes through removing human interaction was one avenue. This required a digitization of processes. Applications and forms were made entirely online. Departmental procedures were merged and streamlined. Close to 1,500 old legislations were identified and scrapped, apart from a vast number of rules, regulations and processes.

Finance Minister Nirmala Sitharaman deserves much credit for pushing these reforms through, as she was Minister of Commerce Industry while I was Secretary (DIPP). Later, as CEO, NITI Aayog, we worked on numerous issues such as disinvestment and asset monetization. I have found her to be one of the most proactive, positive and progressive ministers I have ever worked with. Her file disposal was impeccable. I have never had an occasion where a file was held up in her office. I have always been impressed with her subject matter expertise, intellect and grasp over key policy issues. Now as we build consensus on key global issues during India's G20 presidency, her role will be critical.

As part of the ease of doing business push, we then started ranking states on ease of doing business parameters. This led to healthy competition among state governments in creating an enabling business environment. In the first year, Gujarat came out on top. Andhra Pradesh topped the following year, followed by Telangana in the next. It was heartening to see that states in eastern India, such as Chhattisgarh and Jharkhand, showed significant improvement through the introduction of these reforms. This trend of leveraging competitive federalism has continued at NITI Aayog. We have developed indices on water management, export preparedness, sustainable development goals (SDGs), health and school education, among others. By 2020, India had achieved a rank of 63 in the EoDB rankings, a 79-position improvement in just five years! This again reflects the new attitude through which private enterprise was being viewed.

Our second objective was to attract FDI. First, to simplify processes, the FIPB was abolished in May 2017. Rather than a centralized agency vetting inward FDI approvals, the process of granting approvals has now been left to individual ministries or departments. Several sectors that required approval prior to investment were moved to the automatic route. This meant that no approval from the government was required. Second, the thresholds for automatic investments were raised. For example, in the defence sector, FDI limits were raised to 74 per cent in the automatic route. A similar move was made in the pharmaceuticals sector. Food processing can attract 100 per cent FDI through the automatic route. The broadcasting sector was also opened up to FDI, with limits raised from 49 per cent to 100 per cent in digital cable, for instance. Other sectors with 100 per cent FDI under automatic route include asset reconstruction companies, telecom and railway infrastructure, among others.

Our third objective was introducing a revamped intellectual

property rights (IPR) regime. The process of registration of patents and trademarks was completely revamped and a large number of additional examiners were recruited. The time taken to issue patents has reduced drastically as a result. The new IPR regime has been a key contributor to developing India's innovation ecosystem.

Through these three objectives, the Make in India campaign aimed at improving the capabilities of our domestic firms. The intent of the government was now clear through launching this campaign. Private enterprise would play a leading role in developing India's manufacturing capabilities, while the government would play the role of a facilitator and an enabler. This was a far cry from the view prevalent in the years post-Independence, when the government was envisioned to be at the 'commanding heights of the economy'.

Several policy lessons were also learnt. For domestic and global firms to manufacture in India, cost-competitiveness was the need of the hour. This would be achieved through multisectoral interventions. First, several PLI schemes were introduced to boost size and scale in manufacturing. NITI Aayog has played an important role in the development of these PLI schemes. The strategy incentivizes production rather than provide support on the input side. The key innovation in the PLI schemes is that they incentivize production, and financial outlays are released once targets are met. This is unlike schemes in the past, where financial outlays were made on the input side, such as capital subsidies or interest subvention. By pre-committing investment and production with time-bound targets, the scheme differs substantially in its design. Companies have been selected on the basis of their ability to achieve scale, investment commitments and production levels.

Sectors with the highest potential for growth, exports and employment have been selected. Crucially, the scheme targets sunrise sectors of growth such as advanced chemistry cell (ACC) battery, electronics/technology products and high efficiency solar PV modules. The schemes also target labour-intensive sectors such as textiles, apparel and food processing. Aiming to place India in GVCs, auto and auto components, pharmaceuticals, telecom and networking products, white goods and speciality steel are other sectors for which PLI schemes have been launched. The benefits will not be limited to the companies selected. Take the auto industry as an example. With the rise of domestic manufacturing since liberalization, several Micro, Small and Medium Enterprises (MSMEs) became part of the value chains. Being linked to larger companies helped them grow and raise their productivity and efficiency levels through exposure to newer technologies and management practices. Now, with large PLI schemes launched across various sectors, similar effects can be expected. The objective is to get size and scale in manufacturing to penetrate global markets.

The clarity and policy consistency on offer has been a key feature built into the design of the scheme to encourage investment. This, coupled with the timing of financial outlays, has promoted ease of doing business. Earlier, businesses would have to go through various steps to avail of capital subsidies, for example. The schemes have been enthusiastically received by domestic and foreign investors alike.

The benefits expected to accrue from this scheme are manifold. First, domestic manufacturing will be boosted in sunrise and strategic sectors. By encouraging production, scale is being encouraged in manufacturing, which will lead to cost-competitiveness. Exports are also expected to receive a huge fillip. Assuming an average incentive of 5–6 per cent, the total production from PLI schemes is estimated to be $500 billion over the next few years. Expected investments from these schemes are expected to the tune of $27 billion, generating direct employment for over six million people. Indirect investment and employment, through spurring demand in MSMEs, will further boost our manufacturing capability and domestic demand.

Apart from new schemes, the decision to revise the definition of MSMEs will also help firms grow. As many government schemes exist for the benefit of MSMEs, moving beyond these thresholds meant that these firms would lose the associated benefits. The norms prescribed investment limits that categorized these firms. Separate definitions existed for those engaged in the manufacturing and services sectors. By prescribing investment limits, firms limited investment to remain within the thresholds, hampering productivity growth. For instance, earlier, a micro enterprise was defined as one with investments of less than ₹25 lakh. The new definition raises this threshold to ₹1 crore and adds turnover as an additional criterion. Firms with a turnover of less than ₹5 crore would be identified as micro enterprises. The investment thresholds of small and medium firms have been effectively doubled.

In 2020, the government notified four Labour Codes—the Code on Wages, 2019; the Industrial Relations Code, 2020; the Code on Social Security, 2020; and the Occupational Safety, Health and Working Conditions Code, 2020—which have subsumed 29 Central Labour Laws. Once the rules are framed after due consultations, the laws are expected to boost size and scale in manufacturing and encourage formal employment as well. The much-needed flexibility will be brought in to run operations through these laws, while the rights of workers will remain protected as before.

Another bottleneck in India's value chains was that of infrastructure. For years, India had underinvested in infrastructure. The state of India's transport infrastructure meant that the cost of logistics domestically was higher than in the competing nations. Early on, sector-specific programmes such as Bharatmala (highways), Sagarmala (ports) and UDAN[3] (air travel) were announced. Investments were ramped up for such programmes, with a focus on implementation and timely completion. For instance, the pace of building of National Highways (NHs) increased from 12 kilometres per day in 2014–15 to 37 kilometres per day in 2020–21.[4]

The National Infrastructure Pipeline (NIP) was announced by the PM in his Independence Day speech of 2019. The NIP envisioned investments worth more than ₹100 lakh crore between 2019 and 2025. Crucially, the NIP sees a strong role for the private sector in developing India's infrastructure. Nearly 21 per cent of the total investment is expected to come from the private sector, and the Report of the Task Force on the NIP, of which I was a member, made several key recommendations that would provide an enabling environment for private investments to thrive. Capacity building, optimal risk sharing, adoption of international contract standards and institutionalizing the sanctity and enforcement of contracts were some of the key recommendations made to enable and facilitate greater private-sector participation. This again signalled an important shift in thinking.

To enable better coordination and seamless connectivity among the existing and planned initiatives of various ministries and departments, the PM launched the Gati Shakti Master Plan in his Independence Day speech of 2021. This Master Plan marks another paradigm shift in the governance of infrastructure projects. Departmentalism and working in silos, which was a source of inefficiency, would be tackled by this plan. All existing and proposed economic zones have been mapped along the connectivity

---

[3]Short for 'Ude Desh Ka Aam Nagrik'.
[4]Year-End Review 2021, Ministry of Road Transport and Highways, https://bit. ly/3nKNber, accessed on 8 July 2022.

infrastructure to ensure their connectivity. Furthermore, all future projects will be examined within the parameters of the plan. Achieving an efficient, seamless and multimodal transport network is no easy task. It requires independent government departments to work in close coordination and collaboration, guided by an overarching master plan. This is what Gati Shakti seeks to achieve.

Increasingly, the private sector is being seen as a partner in building India's infrastructure. From physical to social infrastructure, a widening of PPP schemes is evident.

Apart from infrastructure, NITI Aayog has also been working towards increasing the presence of private enterprise in medical education. This unique framework leverages the strengths of both the public and the private sector to create medical colleges in various district hospitals. A model concession agreement for operation and maintenance of electric buses in cities has also been prepared. Interestingly, this model is on an operating expenses (opex) basis, with the private partner expected to undertake the capital expenditure (capex) necessary. The development of logistics parks is also proposed to be undertaken through the PPP mode. Airports are increasingly being developed by the private sector and the highways sector has a long history of successful PPPs.

Governance Redefined

Apart from sector-specific schemes, a focus on governance has not been lost.

Through the Jan Dhan-Aadhaar-Mobile (JAM) trinity, India's governance landscape has been transformed like never before. Bank accounts can now be opened in a matter of seconds. When I was a young officer in Kerala, I was working with the traditional fishing communities. My job was to transform their lives and enhance their livelihoods. We provided them with new fibre glass fishing vessels, outboard motors, and new fishing nets to improve their productivity and economic returns. I recall trying to get bank accounts opened for fishermen; it was an absolute nightmare. It took us 10 months to complete the Know Your Customer (KYC) norms and open those bank accounts!

Between 2015 and 2018, transformative work was done. Close to 460 million bank accounts were opened leveraging Aadhaar under the Pradhan Mantri Jan-Dhan Yojana. Further, close to 55 per cent of all bank accounts opened in the world during this time were opened in India, and 56 per cent of the account holders were women. These accounts were then utilized to directly transfer cash benefits amounting to lakhs of crores directly to beneficiaries, plugging leakages and improving targeting in public expenditure. This was a huge shift. Our investments in financial inclusion meant that during Covid-19, we were able to transfer money directly into the accounts of beneficiaries in a matter of seconds. Contrast this with the US, where Covid-19 relief cheques were being mailed!

After opening bank accounts, the next focus was on digital payments. The PM asked me to drive the digital payments initiative post demonetization. Our team at NITI Aayog worked overnight to find out ways to pay digitally, whether through a smartphone or regular feature phones. We started with a full-page advert in leading newspapers the next day. We created teams of NITI's Young Professionals and lateral entrants, who went around training people and institutions on digital payments. Ranveer made over 50 presentations in the span of a few weeks!

Once we had the basics covered, the PM asked us to hold 100 Digi Dhan Melas in 100 days. We were sceptical about this, and expressed it in a meeting with him. Thankfully, the PM had absolute clarity and overruled us. We then brought together the

National Payments Corporation of India, banks and start-ups and conducted these melas across the country. We leveraged the reach of celebrities to generate momentum. We also distributed prizes—money was directly deposited into the bank accounts of winners. Looking back, these Digi Dhan Melas really set the momentum for digital payments in India. It became a mass movement, as we see today. In retrospect, the PM had a much greater vision than us.

Through the Unified Payments Interface (UPI), digital payment adoption in the country has seen an exponential rise. With the government coming together to provide the underlying data layer, the private sector built solutions on top of it. PhonePe, Google Pay and Paytm, among others, are just some examples. UPI has no doubt been a tremendous success story. To see the scale, in late 2016–17, the year UPI was introduced, total transactions totalled 17.9 million. In September 2022 alone, UPI processed 6.8 billion transactions. Cumulatively, 51 billion transactions have taken place on UPI in 2022. This means that UPI now processes millions of transactions a day, a large chunk of which are peer-to-peer transactions; in other words, cash is being replaced by UPI. As the next step in the evolution, the RBI has opened the retail payment space to further competition. Applications have been invited for a New Umbrella Entity.[5] Several private enterprises have entered the race, according to various reports.[6]

Financial inclusion is just one example of the impact that the 'Digital India' programme has had on governance. Most government

---

[5]Unnikrishnan, Dinesh, 'A "NUE" Rival for NPCI Is in the Making: Why Does the RBI Want Another Entity for Retail Payments?' *Moneycontrol*, 26 February 2021, https://bit.ly/3OMfOUh, accessed on 8 July 2022.
[6]Singh, Ritu, 'Top Banks, Corporates Eye New Umbrella Entity Licence; Last Date to Apply Extended to March 31', *CNBC TV18*, https://bit.ly/3zYvjnC, accessed on 23 June 2022.

services have been brought online and made Aadhaar enabled. Digital versions of important documents like Aadhaar, Permanent Account Number, driving licence, etc., can be stored online, through DigiLocker, under which documents stored are deemed equivalent to physical copies. All government services have also been brought onto a single app called UMANG (Unified Mobile Application for New-Age Governance). Massive investments in setting up the tech backbone have enabled India to take a leap forward in the new economy.

Transformation at the Grassroots

Mahasamund in Chhattisgarh, Kiphire in Nagaland, Mamit in Mizoram, Kandhamal in Odisha and Lohardaga in Jharkhand are geographically far-flung districts in India, whose names you have probably not even heard of. Suffering for years on account of poor governance, transforming India's 112 backward districts, through the Aspirational Districts Programme (ADP), has been a key priority. Launched by the PM in January 2018, the ADP seeks to improve socio-economic outcomes by reimagining governance, vesting greater ownership and accountability in the district administration, facilitating convergence and collaboration among stakeholders within and outside the government, ensuring tracking of performance indicators on a real-time basis as well as engaging citizens to contribute to the development process. Since its launch, all 112 underdeveloped districts included in the programme have improved their performance. While some have surpassed the state averages on key indicators, many Aspirational Districts are now the best performing of all districts in the state. Take Dantewada, for example, with 35 of the districts under forest cover and infamous for being part of the Red Corridor. The progress since 2018 has been astonishing. The Shri Atal Bihari

Vajpayee Education City in the district houses 18 educational institutions and has brought down insurgency rates. Tribal women are now driving autorickshaws. The state-of-the-art district hospital in Baramulla or the complete electrification of Kupwara are some of the other success stories.

The broad contours of the ADP are Convergence (of central and state schemes), Collaboration (of central, state-level Prabhari officers and district collectors) and Competition among districts through monthly delta ranking ('3Cs' approach), driven by a mass movement ('Jan Andolan'). Aligned with a broad framework developed by NITI Aayog, district-level vision and action plans have been drawn up. These plans are based on a thorough analysis of the strengths and weaknesses of every district.

To empower government officials who are closest to the ground in making decisions without having to wait for authorities at higher levels, district collectors have been designated as the focal points of this programme. They play a critical role in implementing and monitoring initiatives, based on the continuously evolving reality of their districts as captured on a dashboard.

One of the most powerful drivers of the programme has been the focus on leveraging technology, real-time data, and a robust monitoring and evaluation mechanism. Under the ADP, key performance indicators (KPIs) have been identified on which progress is monitored on a real-time basis through the 'Champions of Change' platform. This enables government officials to make the requisite course corrections in programme implementation. It also spurs competition among districts by allowing them to regularly assess their position vis-à-vis other Aspirational Districts as well as the best-performing district in the country.

A baseline ranking of all Aspirational Districts was released by NITI Aayog in April 2018, based on published data of 49 indicators. The KPIs were identified following detailed consultations with relevant government ministries and knowledge partners. These are primarily socio-economic outcomes in health and nutrition, education, agriculture and irrigation, financial inclusion, skill development and basic infrastructure. To empower field officers, NITI Aayog prepared a primer mapping the 49 KPIs with existing schemes and listing specific actionable steps for improving the district's performance on every indicator. The districts are ranked on the basis of improvements from the baseline and the latest ranking on monthly progress (delta) is announced by NITI Aayog.

The strategy is already bearing fruit. For example, in the critical indicator of having pregnant women registered for antenatal check-ups within the first trimester, the Lohardaga district in Jharkhand had a baseline value of 43.9 per cent around the start of the programme. The district's current value is above 90 per cent. Similarly, the Namsai district of Arunachal Pradesh, which started off in the programme at 21 per cent institutional deliveries, will soon be reaching 100 per cent value. In the Kondagaon district of Chhattisgarh, compared to 35.9 per cent schools meeting the Right to Education pupil teacher ratio (in 2018), today, in 2022, close of 100 per cent schools are meeting it.

The success achieved by the ADP has been globally recognized. The United Nations Development Programme (UNDP) has appreciated the programme's '3Cs' principle and recommended its replication in other parts of the developing world. In their appraisal of the ADP, it noted that ADP is 'a very successful model of local area development' that 'should serve as a best practice for several other countries where regional disparities in development status persist for many reasons.'[7]

Several independent experts have also lauded the programme's

[7]'UNDP Report Lauds Aspirational Districts Programme, Recommends Replication in Other Parts of the World', NITI Aayog, 11 June 2021, https://bit.ly/3NgDJd5, accessed on 23 June 2022.

success in catalysing rapid improvements in performance in the areas of health, nutrition, education and infrastructure. Prof. Michael E. Porter, Harvard Business School, has opined that, 'True success requires the integration of competitiveness and social progress... The 2018 launch of the "Transformation of the Aspirational Districts" program (TADP)" has been a bold and promising strategic step towards this new agenda.'[8]

Further, by opening its doors to the private sector, philanthropic organizations and technical partners, the ADP is changing the deeply entrenched popular perception that development is, to a large extent, the prerogative of the government alone. These partnerships are helping infuse the programme with new ideas and acting as force multipliers on outcomes.

These development partners include Piramal Foundation facilitating improvements in education, health and nutrition; MicroSave driving financial inclusion; ITC Ltd driving interventions in agriculture; L&T improving skill development; Tata Trusts specifically working collaboratively in LWE-affected districts; and IDinsight acting as a third-party evaluator, to name a few. These development partners have worked extensively with district administrations, driving constructive action, and focussing on building the capacity of district officials to improve governance at the district level. Their actions have not just been limited to the district level. During Covid, through the ADP, we were able to reach the hyper-local level as well.

For example, NITI Aayog, in partnership with Piramal Foundation, launched an innovative Surakshit Dada-Dadi, Nana-Nani Abhiyaan, with the objective of addressing the vulnerabilities of senior citizens during Covid. Starting with 25 districts, the campaign was scaled up to all 112 aspirational districts. In

---

[8]'Foreword by Michael Porter & Scott Stern', Institute for Competitiveness, https://bit.ly/3xRFGqJ, accessed on 23 June 2022.

partnership with district administrations, NGOs led this campaign in their respective districts. During this time, more than 29 lakhs senior citizens were supported by 1.4 lakh Apne Saathi volunteers. Senior citizens' issues, such as lack of food, medicines or banking services, were resolved by 151 NGOs providing virtual care.

With the success of this campaign, the Surakshit Hum Surakshit Tum Abhiyaan was launched to address vaccine hesitancy. The programme ensured the vaccination of over 22 lakh people across the Aspirational Districts. Having worked closely with Piramal Foundation during my time as CEO, I can speak first-hand of the phenomenal work they have done in the spheres of health and education. I would like to compliment Ajay and Swati Piramal for their passion and commitment. They closely collaborated with NITI Aayog in improving the Aspirational Districts, making a difference in learning and health outcomes and eradicating tuberculosis. Partnerships such as these exemplify the new paradigm of governance in India.

The programme has also demonstrated that good governance, based on real-time data, constant competition, motivation of staff and rankings in public domain make a huge difference in performance. The programme is now being spread to additional districts and the model of data-based governance is being replicated at the block level, too.

Clearly, data can have a transformational role to play in development and in reducing poverty. However, data must be accessible, in the public domain and be generated in real time. While we are generating vast amounts of data, we are also putting in mechanisms to analyse data and bring out actionable insights. The indices developed at NITI Aayog are one example. The National Data and Analytics Platform is another example. Ensuring data quality is another important aspect. The Data Governance Quality Index, and data quality interventions in the

ADP are building India's capability in data systems. We created dashboards to put all of this data in the public domain. Without data, there can be no improvement in our outcomes.

Disinvestment and Privatization

Focussing on governance issues also brought a renewed vigour in the governance of central public sector enterprises (CPSEs). For years, the management of these enterprises was crying out for reform. The issues with the banking system, especially in PSBs, partly resulted from outdated and inefficient management practices. Rather than returning surpluses to the government as originally envisioned, the years since Independence saw many CPSEs drain public resources rather than contribute to them. This is not to say all public enterprises were a drain on resources. However, many loss-making CPSEs continued to receive support. Plans for revival were drawn up many times; however, they rarely came to fruition.

Disinvestment and privatization, a process that was initiated in the early 2000s and had effectively stalled towards the end of the 2000s and early 2010s, returned to the centre stage. A new policy on strategic disinvestment of CPSEs was announced in the Budget Speech of 2015. NITI Aayog has played a leading role in this regard, tasked with identifying CPSEs for disinvestment, and advising the government on the mode of sale and percentage of shares to be sold as well as methods to value these CPSEs.

This again marked a paradigm shift in the way the private sector was viewed. It represented a recognition that handing over management and control to private enterprises would result in these firms becoming more efficient and productive. In 2021, the Cabinet approved a new PSE Policy. Under this policy, a clear distinction was made between strategic and non-strategic sectors.

Under the new policy, PSEs in non-strategic sectors are expected to be privatized or closed down. Even in strategic sectors, efforts would be made to reduce the number of PSEs involved. This again represents a huge shift in the thinking of the government. From the 1950s, when practically every sector was kept reserved or saw a role from the government, the list has been pared down considerably since then. The sale of Air India is perhaps the best example of this new view within the government. A long and arduous process saw Air India returned to its original owners, the Tata Group.

The Budget of 2021–22 announced the privatization of two PSBs. When I was NITI Aayog CEO, we identified the banks to be privatized after detailed deliberations. I believe the process needs to be carried out in a phased manner. The idea is to broad base holding of equity where the public owns an increasing share. Government holdings can be brought down to less than 50 per cent and the management professionalized. In this new digital era, the transformation of PSBs is necessary. Otherwise, the risk of value erosion is high.

Mining is another area that became the domain of the government after coal mines were nationalized in the 1970s. While private participation gradually increased, the mining sector continued to be plagued with policy inconsistency. First, no clear policy existed at the central level for allocation of coal mines. In 2014, the Supreme Court ruled that all the licences granted for mining between 1993 and 2010 stood cancelled, after a report published by the Comptroller and Auditor General of India. It was clear that a new direction was needed in mining. Despite holding one of the highest reserves in the world, India remained a net importer of coal.

NITI Aayog played a decisive role in this regard as well. A High-Level Committee, led by NITI Aayog, made several ground-breaking recommendations. The coal sector was proposed to be liberalized and opened to private enterprise, while maintaining transparency. Crucially, we at NITI Aayog recommended that rather than trying to maximize revenue, the goal should be to maximize production. This would incentivize production and spur growth and employment. Private enterprise would bring in investments and efficiencies and boost the overall productivity of India's coal sector. Commercial mining with regulatory oversight can enrich local communities as well, as the case with Hindustan Zinc has shown. The local population has benefitted immensely, through investments in infrastructure. Moreover, the traditions and customs of the tribal communities remain protected as well.

In infrastructure, it was also increasingly being recognized that while the public sector can build infrastructure, it is often unable to run it efficiently. The private sector, on the other hand, can bring in the much-needed efficiencies in the running of such infrastructure assets. Given that India has one of the largest brownfield stock of fixed assets, mechanisms were needed to be developed so that these assets could be utilized to their full potential. At the same time, India's PPP framework has matured considerably. Much has been learned from the institutional mechanisms, model contract frameworks, standards and financing through the evolution of PPPs in India. It was seen that while the private sector had shown an appetite for developing greenfield projects, there remained an untapped opportunity in brownfield projects. There is increased evidence of private capital flowing into infrastructure sectors such as roads, power and telecommunications.

This was the idea behind asset monetization, which, simply put, allows the government to monetize underperforming assets, without giving up ownership. This makes it different from privatization. Under asset monetization, assets such as roads and transmission grids, among others, can be transferred to the private sector (through a competitive process) for them to run, manage and monetize. The notion that these assets are being 'sold off' to the private sector is, therefore, entirely unfounded. The goal of asset monetization is to unlock value from public investment in infrastructure.

Accordingly, in July 2019, the GoI unveiled an ambitious asset monetization pipeline over five years. There have been several success stories. The National Highways Authority of India has monetized toll roads to the tune of approx. ₹15,000 crore by January 2021 through the toll-operate-transfer model. Similarly, in May 2021, the Power Grid Corporation of India completed the monetization of the first batch of its transmission assets, fetching ₹7,700 crore. The Airports Authority of India has successfully monetized six brownfield airports through the operation management and development agreement.

Based on the mandate for asset monetization under the Union Budget 2021–22, NITI Aayog developed the National Monetisation Pipeline (NMP). It was launched by Finance Minister Nirmala Sitharaman in July 2021 and envisaged a target of ₹6 lakh crore of monetization between FYs 2022 and 2025. The government garnered ₹96,000 crore under the NMP in FY 2022, surpassing the target of ₹88,000 crore. Coal mining, roads, minerals and power were the key sectors where assets were monetized. The cumulative potential of the assets monetized in FY 2022 is in excess of ₹9 lakh crore. The programme has led to new models such as infrastructure investment trusts (InvITs) and real estate investment trusts (REITs) being implemented in India. REITs are a finance vehicle that owns and manages properties that generate regular income. They function just like mutual funds. They pool money from investors and provide them with an easy entry point in markets. They can also be listed on stock exchanges. InvITs function in a similar way, except that they invest in infrastructure projects that generate cash flows. They provide a steady stream of income through dividends and long-term capital appreciation.

Private Sector as a Partner

The discussion around disinvestment, privatization, PPP and asset monetization is reflective of the evolved view of the private sector that has now firmly been established in the government. The strengths of the public and the private sector are now being complemented to ensure India's growth and prosperity. In fact, India's growth story will now be led by the private sector, with the government playing the role of an enabler and a facilitator. However, this expanded role for the private sector entails more. One example comes from the 'Champions of Change' event organized by NITI Aayog in 2017. Spread over two weekends, start-ups and young entrepreneurs were invited by NITI to deliberate on key policy issues. Over 400 young entrepreneurs and founders of start-ups attended this event. Twelve economic sectors were covered and a road map prepared, which was then presented to PM Modi. Issues such as agriculture, manufacturing, infrastructure, cities of tomorrow, Digital India and education, among others, were covered during this event.

The PM spent an enormous amount of time interacting with the young entrepreneurs. Supported by young policy analysts from NITI, the exercise was entirely driven and led by the private sector. They deliberated over the weekend on key policy issues and drew actionable policy recommendations across the entire gamut of the Indian economy.

The process did not end with the event. Regular government-to-business (G2B) dialogue was enabled and sectoral working groups created in line ministries. The policymaking process was most definitely enriched through these interactions. NITI, in turn, regularly collaborates with these founders/entrepreneurs on a range of issues. For instance, in the months following Champions of Change, NITI Aayog extensively consulted with these invitees during the preparation of the *Strategy for New India @ 75* document. Since then, NITI regularly reaches out to these entrepreneurs on a range of issues. I have termed these entrepreneurs the 'intellectual think tanks' of NITI Aayog. Furthermore, the intent of the government to listen to and appreciate inputs and concerns shared by the private sector was widely acknowledged as a positive signal.

That the public and private sector are now working closely together has been best exemplified during India's Covid-19 response. In the initial days of Covid in 2020, the private sector worked to ensure that most PPE (personal protective equipment) kits, masks and testing kits were made in India. This ensured vital supply at a crucial time. Vaccines were a key component of the global Covid management strategy. Again, Indian companies came to the fore. Take the role played by Serum Institute of India (SII), led by Adar Poonawalla. SII manufactured millions of vaccine doses, ensuring an adequate supply during a time of peak demand, playing a crucial role in stemming the Covid tide. This did not happen by accident. In the years leading up to the pandemic, Poonawalla had led SII in building their technological and manufacturing capacity. This speaks to his risk-taking ability and foresight. I personally visited the SII factory along with Poonawalla and was left thoroughly impressed. He has played a crucial role in making India the vaccine capital of the world.

During Covid, India developed four indigenous vaccines in two years. Covaxin, India's first vaccine, which was another major milestone in our vaccination journey, was developed by Bharat Biotech and the Indian Council for Medical Research

(ICMR). Bharat Biotech also launched iNCOVACC, the world's first intranasal Covid vaccine. India was also the first country in the world to approve a DNA-based vaccine developed by Zydus. The world's first mRNA vaccine, Gemcovac-19, was developed by Gennova Biopharmaceuticals. Corbevax was licensed to the Indian firm Biological E for manufacturing. Without these efforts by Indian companies, the vaccination story of India, and indeed the world, would have been very different.

While it was acknowledged that the private sector would have a leading role to play in the development of the nation, we also see a renewed thrust towards innovation and entrepreneurship. While the power of entrepreneurship had been unleashed in the years following the reforms of 1991, a robust innovation ecosystem had been missing from India. Bengaluru had emerged as an IT hub, but India's start-up ecosystem remained relatively small. Indian engineers found employment in droves, but the best talent was still hesitant towards entrepreneurship. Even though the quality of Indian engineering was lauded, most innovation and entrepreneurship occurred in the business-to-business (B2B) and business-to-government (B2G) segments. Indian companies were building robust software solutions for some of the biggest companies in the world. However, the most innovative firms in the West, such as Google, which was founded as recently as 1998, and Amazon, were not just in the B2B market but also in the business-to-consumer (B2C) market. Indian companies and entrepreneurs were not building products for consumers yet.

There were only a handful of successes exemplified most notably by Sanjeev Bikhchandani, who set up InfoEdge in 1995 and launched Naukri.com in 1997. Within a few years, Naukri was one of India's leading employment websites. In 2006, Naukri.com listed on the BSE and NSE and was oversubscribed by over

55 times.[9] However, this journey was no easy task. Funding for start-ups at that time was rare. Venture capital was just about entering India's financial lexicon. Capital was available from banks, but they would hardly lend to a new business, given the hoops an established business had to jump through in the 1990s. In a feature published in *Forbes* magazine, Bikhchandani recalls he had to wait six months to get a working capital loan from a PSB in the early 1990s.[10] For the first few years, he worked without a salary, keeping costs down and the company afloat.

A pioneer in setting up internet-based companies in India, Bikhchandani has paved the way for numerous other internet start-ups, like jeevansathi.com, which is another early example of an internet-based business built in India. However, such examples were still rare in the 1990s to late 2000s. Global recognition of India as a hub of innovation was still missing. It was clear that a culture shift was needed, not just in colleges but also in schools. Innovative and out-of-the-box thinking had to be inculcated from a young age. The power of start-ups had to be unleashed and harnessed.

[9] Thaker, Naini, 'Sanjeev Bikhchandani: From Pioneer to Messiah of India's Internet Startups', *Forbes India*, 30 August 2021, https://bit.ly/3ABs8Tc, accessed on 8 July 2022.
[10] Ibid.

SIX

UPSTARTS:
THE WORLD OF START-UPS

On 16 January 2016, PM Modi launched a flagship initiative intended to catalyse the start-up culture and build a strong and inclusive ecosystem for innovation and entrepreneurship in India. It was called Startup India. As secretary (DIPP), I was tasked with the launch of this mission. The PM wanted a whole-of-government approach. Every ministry was involved. A complete start-up action plan was put together. At this point in time, India had a lot of regulatory cholesterol. The same laws and regulations that applied to the industry would have been applicable to start-ups, which would have choked their growth. We wanted to ensure ease of doing business for start-ups. But for that, ministries needed to come up with a definition. This was an extremely challenging task, given the dynamic nature of the start-up ecosystem. However, in consultation with various stakeholders, we came up with a definition for start-ups. They would be exempt from many labour laws, including at the state level. Those who wanted income tax exemptions could avail of them for a block of four years in the first seven.

At the launch of Startup India, we had a line-up of stellar speakers. We had delegations from Silicon Valley visit and speak at the event. We ensured only start-up founders would share the dais with the PM. The selfie taken by the start-up founders with the PM exemplified the new energy and vitality that this movement brought to India. Nobody had envisaged such an overwhelming response.

The past few years have seen India's innovation ecosystem both expand and mature at the same time. Combined with an enabling economic environment, India's start-up ecosystem is now a world leader. Taking a journey through some numbers shows how far this ecosystem has come. Clearly, the evidence is irrefutable. Since 2015, we have seen a nine-time increase in the number of investors, a seven-time increase in the number of incubators and a 15-time increase in the total funding of start-ups.[1] Since the launch of Startup India, approx. 65,000 start-ups have been officially recognized. In a recently released report, NASSCOM and Zinnov revealed that almost 25,000–26,000 tech start-ups were founded in India between 2011 and 2021.[2] In 2021, we added three to four new 'unicorns' every month. India's start-up ecosystem is now the third largest in the world. A new internet user is being added every three seconds. Seventy-five crore or 750 million people are accessing the internet every day.

India has all the right ingredients to create world-leading companies in this new economy, which is digital and green. Our investments in tertiary education and strong STEM (Science, Technology, Engineering and Mathematics) education, combined with entrepreneurial zeal and innovation, will catapult India to a new era. We not only have the manpower but also one of the largest markets in the world. Our middle class already numbers in the hundreds of millions, and is only likely to grow in the future, both in terms of size and purchasing power.

This success has not come by accident. Public policy has increasingly placed innovation and entrepreneurship at the top of its agenda. Through landmark initiatives such as Startup India, a revamped IPR regime and interventions in education, innovation is truly being democratized in India. As per NASSCOM, 29 per cent of all tech start-ups in India are now coming up in the emerging start-up hubs of Ahmedabad, Kolkata, Indore, Lucknow, Coimbatore, Chandigarh and Jaipur, among others.[3]

---

[1]'Startup Ecosystem in India: The Indian Unicorn Landscape', *Invest India*, https://bit.ly/3ySal93, accessed on 7 July 2022.
[2]'Startups Raised More Than Rs 1.79 Lakh Crore in 2021, Says Nasscom-Zinnov Report', Scroll.in, 22 January 2022, https://bit.ly/3RPeL6Y, accessed on 11 September 2022.
[3]NASSCOM and Zinnov, *NASSCOM Tech Start-Up Report 2021: Year of the Titans*, https://bit.ly/3RQ0FDh, accessed on 21 July 2022.

In 2021, 40 per cent of all start-ups founded came from these emerging hubs, rather than the traditional ones, the report reveals. Lendingkart, DeHaat and BluSmart Mobility are just some of the top funded start-ups in these emerging hubs.

We increasingly see women take on the roles of founders as well. Ghazal Alagh, for example, is the co-founder of the beauty brand MamaEarth. Ruchi Deepak co-founded Acko Insurance. NITI Aayog has also been taking the lead in creating a platform of women entrepreneurs through the Women Entrepreneurship Platform.

India's start-ups are now solving some of the most pressing issues faced by India. E-commerce may have driven the first wave, but now we see companies innovating in areas such as finance (fintech), agriculture (agritech), health (health-tech) and education (edtech), among others. Take the evolution of India's fintech industry, for instance. As a result of the Digital India mission, the JAM Trinity of Jan-Dhan accounts, hundreds of millions of mobile phones and Aadhaar cards, most households in India now have access to basic banking services. India Stack, with APIs such as Aadhaar authentication, eKYC, eSign and UPI, has allowed governments and businesses to utilize the public digital infrastructure to offer financial services and accelerate the adoption of cashless behaviour. Unified Payments Interface, for instance, has become a way of life for millions. The government's approach of developing platforms, rather than products, is paying dividends. World-class products are being developed by the private sector, on top of public digital infrastructure. Now, from digital payments, the focus is shifting to digital lending.

Right from BHIM, Paytm, PhonePe and Google Pay to Amazon Pay, numerous apps are facilitating payments with the click of a button. Innovations in this space have allowed new models of lending to come up that look at cash flows, rather than assets.

Lendingkart, Pine Labs and MobiKwik are some of the start-ups operating in this space. With sufficient comfort with payments and lending, there has been an increased focus towards personal finance, money management, investments and trading. A plethora of top-class entities have come up in this space. Zerodha, Groww and Upstox are some examples. They have created an ecosystem of modern investment apps. We are now witnessing the emergence of financial products that target the more complex segments. For instance, the new insurance tech companies such as Digit and Acko are greatly simplifying the insurance market. They cover the entire cycle of origination, undertaking, claims and selection.

Digital investment and wealth-management apps are showing phenomenal growth. India has mastered digital payments as other countries continue to struggle. Now, we have moved on to the next step—insurance, investments and wealth management. Indian companies are poised to become world leaders in this space. The business models being developed in Indian markets are now finding global recognition. I am a firm believer that it is only through technological interventions that we will be able to solve India's festering problems.

Start-ups with tech-based platforms are also giving rise to the gig economy in India. Flexible working hours and project-based work are creating a million entrepreneurs in India—be they blue-collar workers or white. Both domestic as well as international platforms are providing such opportunities.

Many start-ups started their initial public offerings (IPOs) process in 2021. Zomato, Nykaa, Policybazaar and Paytm are notable examples. This is an important signal to both domestic and international investors on the maturity of India's start-up ecosystem. With a robust digital infrastructure in place, powered through the Digital India mission and a maturing innovation ecosystem, India is poised to take the next step in the technological revolution.

Through leveraging deep-tech, which includes technologies such as AI, ML, augmented reality (AR)-virtual reality (VR), internet of things (IoT), blockchain, robotics, big data and drones, among others, India's start-ups can lead the nation into a new era of growth and prosperity.

The Rise of Unicorns

The year 2021 has truly been all about the rise of unicorns in India. That year saw 44 unicorns being created, with a combined valuation in excess of $90 billion. This was on the back of 11 unicorns in 2020 and seven in 2019.[4] As of September 2022, India was home to 107 such unicorns, with a total valuation of over $340.79 billion. The year 2022 saw the addition of 21 unicorns in India. This is a huge difference from 2016 or 2017, when one new unicorn emerged every year.

NASSCOM's report reveals some important facts about the unicorns that emerged in 2021. The average age of these unicorns was six years, 40 per cent served global markets and 62 per cent were selling directly to consumers. In addition, the unicorns created in 2021 were spread across 18 sectors. The year saw unicorns come up in areas such as cryptocurrency, e-grocery, social commerce, health-tech, professional services and manufacturing. A combination of thriving digital payments, considerable penetration of smartphones and digital-first business models drove the rise of unicorns in 2021, according to *Invest India*. This view has also been echoed by NASSCOM and other publications.

InMobi was India's first unicorn, attaining the status in 2011, after being founded in 2007. Flipkart attained the unicorn status in 2012. In 2014, it bought Myntra, in one of the biggest

---

[4]'Startup Ecosystem in India: The Indian Unicorn Landscape', *Invest India*, https://bit.ly/3ySal93, accessed on 7 July 2022.

e-commerce deals India had seen, to enter the fashion segment, and thereafter acquired PhonePe in 2016, entering the payments space. Grown by Indian entrepreneurs, Sachin and Binny Bansal, Flipkart has been going toe to toe with the global giant Amazon in India's e-commerce market even before being acquired by the global retail giant, Walmart, in 2018. The year 2015 saw a flurry of activity, with companies such as Paytm, Ola, Quikr, Snapdeal and Zomato joining the club. Now, we have more emerging every month. Apart from a higher number of unicorns being created, start-ups are also reaching this milestone faster. According to Inc42, start-ups founded before 2011 took seven years to achieve unicorn status. However, start-ups founded after 2012 took an average of five years.[5]

Further, these unicorns are not limited to the sectors in which they operate, as mentioned by Credit Suisse in a report published in 2021.[6] This study informed us that India by then was already home to 100-plus unicorns.[7] Neelkanth Mishra, who led the development of the report, stated that unicorns in India were functioning in sectors such as pharmaceuticals, biotechnology, consumer goods and other tech-enabled sectors. Rising formalization of the economy and a strong digital backbone were key enablers, according to him.

Clearly, Indian start-ups and entrepreneurs were not confining themselves to sectors such as IT, software development and app development, among others, in which we had a long-established competitive advantage. Entrepreneurs were now venturing into

---

[5]Sil, Debarghya, 'Indian Startups Are Becoming Unicorn One Year Faster in 2021', Inc42, 10 December 2021, https://bit.ly/3al74pl, accessed on 7 July 2022.
[6]For a full list, see 'Venture Intelligence Unicorn Tracker', Venture Intelligence, https://bit.ly/3OYVFKY, accessed on 7 July 2022.
[7]'India's 100-Strong Unicorn Club Drives Radical Change in the Country's Corporate Landscape', Credit Suisse Asian Investment Conference, Credit Suisse, 23 March 2020, https://bit.ly/3ImetRA, accessed on 7 July 2022.

new areas, confident in their abilities to solve a problem and create a market. They are disrupting markets way ahead of traditional players and shaking the status quo.

In the healthcare segment, we saw Innovaccer become the first Indian unicorn in this space. PharmEasy was the second. Cure.fit, too, joined the club by November 2021. In the fintech space, among others, Cred, Groww, BharatPe, Upstox and Acko achieved unicorn status in 2021. Several software as a service (SaaS) start-ups such as BrowserStack and Chargebee joined the club. India also has a rapidly evolving edtech space led by Byju's, which attained unicorn status in 2018. Vedantu, Eruditus and upGrad were further entrants from edtech in the list in 2021. Licious, a direct-to-consumer supplier of meat and poultry products, is another example. Urban Company, which has transformed the personal services segment, achieved unicorn status in 2021.

An article by Ken Koyanagi in *Nikkei Asia* reveals the extent to which markets are being transformed in India.[8] Zetwerk has brought manufacturing good suppliers and subcontractors on to a platform where they can access markets both nationally and internationally. OfBusiness has created a platform for industrial materials, connecting buyers and sellers of cement, steel and grains, among others. Blackbuck is matching demand and supply in the truck transport business, another area which has traditionally been dominated by the informal sector.

Undoubtedly, India is an extremely exciting place to be. After the US and China, we have the highest number of unicorns. By developing innovative products, start-ups are able to access India's vast market and grow exponentially. This rise of B2B platforms and start-ups has the potential for Indian MSMEs to break away from their low-productivity, low-growth trap. They

[8]Koyanagi, Ken, 'India's Unicorn Boom Shows No Signs of Slowdown', *Nikkei Asia*, 16 September 2021, https://s.nikkei.com/3yOkcfX, accessed on 7 July 2022.

now have access to sophisticated operations with information at their fingertips. This certainly bodes exceedingly well for India's future growth prospects, especially for its 6.3 crore-plus MSMEs.

Pinnacle of Start-Up Success

Apart from being known as the year of unicorns, 2021 will also be remembered as the year of IPOs in India's start-up community. Some of the notable companies to file their IPOs included Zomato, Paytm, Nykaa, Policybazaar and Map My India. Overall, 11 tech start-ups were listed in domestic and global markets. According to the *NASSCOM Tech Start-Up Report 2021,* $6.2 billion was raised by these start-ups during their listing, with a cumulative market capitalization of $47.8 billion. These IPOs were oversubscribed by 67 times, showing the level of interest generated in both institutional and retail investors. Perhaps importantly, many of the start-ups are now going in for domestic listing rather than foreign. There are several benefits to listing domestically rather than in outside markets. The growing presence of retail investors, along with a strong base of institutional investors, both domestic and foreign, means the pool of funds accessible in India's capital markets is much larger than it was a few decades ago. The fact that many of India's start-ups are now maturing and entering the IPO stage bodes well for India's start-up and innovation ecosystem. We also see increased corporate presence in the start-up ecosystem.

As per NASSCOM, 2021 saw 260 plus corporate deals, a 1.5 time increase since 2020. Both Indian and global MNCs participated in equal measure. While there were several M&As, collaboration has emerged as an important theme. NASSCOM highlights some examples. For example, PayU Money and Kreditech launched a 'cardless' EMI system. Sastra Robotics has partnered with Bosch to automate the testing of devices. Corporates are also increasingly promoting start-up programmes through open innovation, incubators, accelerators, ecosystem outreach and partner programmes.

M&As have played an important role in India's maturing start-up and innovation ecosystem. Early examples include Flipkart acquiring Myntra in 2014 and then PhonePe in 2016. Ola is another example. It acquired TaxiForSure in 2015 and Foodpanda in 2017. Zomato acquired the US-based competitor Urbanspoon in 2015, giving it a global presence. Byjus's has also been on an acquiring spree. Most notably, it bought Aakash Educational Services in 2021 for a deal worth $1 billion. This also marks the time when digital-first businesses started making deals in the offline space. BharatPe, operating in the payments space, together with Centrum Finance is reported to have agreed to take over the operations of Punjab and Maharashtra Cooperative Bank, which had been under an RBI moratorium. This is perhaps a first, where a payments company is acquiring a bank. PharmEasy acquired a global diagnostics company in a deal worth $613 million to enter the diagnostics segment.

Overall, 2021 also witnessed a flurry of activity in the M&As' space. According to reports, 2021 saw M&A deals increase by 137 per cent from 2020.[9] In fact, the number of deals was at an all-time high in 2021, as analysis by *Inc42* shows. E-commerce led the pack in terms of acquisitions, but edtech and fintech companies were not far behind. An increasing trend towards 'Thrasio-style' start-ups is also seen, according to *Inc42*. Named after an American start-up called Thrasio, its business model was founded on acquiring several B2C brands and helping them scale further. In India, companies such as GlobalBees, Mensa Brands

---

[9]Sil, D, 'In Review: Here Is the List of Top Startup Acquisitions & the Top Acquirers of the Year', *Inc42*, 24 December 2021, https://bit.ly/3AyptcX, accessed on 7 July 2022.

and Curefoods are just a few examples of companies that went on an acquiring spree in 2021.

The start-up ecosystem witnessed both an expansion in funding and investors in 2021. For instance, 2019 saw 1,175 deals across all stages of funding. In 2021, the total number of deals stood at 1,412, as analysis by NASSCOM shows. Of note are two other findings from the report. First, compared to 2020, the number of deals at the seed stage saw a two-time increase. Second, in terms of quantum of funding, 2021 saw a two-time increase in late-stage funding compared to 2019. The increase in late-stage deals indicates that many start-ups are now maturing and set to achieve scale in their operations, ahead of potential IPOs. The two-time increase in seed funding compared to 2020 tells us that the entrepreneurial zeal of Indians is only beginning to be tapped. Between 2020 and 2021, the number of corporate investors and venture capital funds nearly doubled.

What is interesting to see is that many former and current founders of start-ups are increasingly looking out for new and innovative companies to invest in. Sanjeev Bikhchandani is probably a pioneer in this space. Back in 2010, InfoEdge invested ₹4.7 crore as seed money in Zomato. When Zomato went public in 2021, InfoEdge earned a dazzling 1,000 time return on their investment![10] InfoEdge also made substantial gains when Policybazaar went public the same year. However, we also saw existing start-ups actively invest in other start-ups. Again, 2021 proved to be a year of change. NASSCOM's start-up report reveals that Zerodha was one of the most active investors in 2021, making four deals. Razorpay, PharmEasy and Shiprocket, among others, became investors as well. In fact, many start-ups

---

[10]Shah, Sneha, 'Info Edge Clocks a Return of 1,050 Times on Zomato Investment', *The Economic Times*, 24 July 2021, https://bit.ly/3NPPIOP, accessed on 7 July 2022.

are now running their own incubation programmes. The entry of new institutional investors in both early stage and late-stage funding rounds reiterates the fact that India's start-up ecosystem is only getting started.

Now, start-ups and entrepreneurs in India are ready to ride the next technological wave. Frontier technologies, such as AI, ML, AR-VR, IoT, blockchain, robotics, big data and drones, among others, collectively make up what is colloquially known as Industry 4.0. NITI Aayog has been at the forefront in helping create an innovative ecosystem for these new technologies to thrive. We see increased evidence of young Indians building solutions and products in this space. For instance, the Bharat Innovation Fund, backed by IIM-Ahmedabad's Centre for Innovation Incubation and Entrepreneurship, has funded seven deep-tech start-ups. Solutions employing technologies such as AI-ML, natural language processing (NLP), AR-VR and drones are being developed by the start-ups funded by the Bharat Innovation Fund. CreditVidya uses AI-ML techniques to devise credit scores. Similarly, India DeepTech, a pan-industry alliance, selected its first cohort for its accelerator programme. Among themselves, these start-ups are involved in areas such as robotics, biotechnology, genomics and cyber-security. A report in *The Times of India* noted that the funding for deep-tech start-ups doubled between 2020 and 2021.[11]

Building an Innovation Ecosystem

The role of the 'Startup India' initiative in promoting India's start-up ecosystem cannot be underestimated. The programme has taken a multifaceted approach in building a strong ecosystem for nurturing innovation and entrepreneurship. The Startup India

---

[11]Hariharan, Sindhu, 'Funding to Deep Tech Startups Doubles in 2021', *The Times of India*, 25 December 2021, https://bit.ly/3yrl08W, accessed on 7 July 2022.

portal connects start-ups, investors, funds, mentors, incubators, accelerators, corporates, academics and policymakers. By December 2020, more than 4.5 lakh registrations were seen on this portal. More than two lakh queries have been attended to and close to three lakh start-ups have accessed the training and learning modules available on the portal.

The portal was just one component. Perhaps more importantly, the regulatory framework was altered like never before as a result of the Startup India programme. A self-certification-based compliance system was introduced for most environment and labour laws. Rebates in registration fees for patents and trademarks were made available. The IPR system in itself was transformed. A Whole-of-Government Approach meant that regulators such as SEBI issued simplified regulations for investors and start-ups. The RBI eased incoming foreign investment regulations as well. Public procurement norms were also simplified and relaxed so that start-ups could participate. Tax holidays were also announced. The National Startup Advisory Council, notified in 2020, was tasked with advising the government on key policy issues related to innovation and start-ups. A 'fund of funds' for start-ups worth ₹10,000 crore was established in 2016. A Startup India seed fund scheme was introduced in 2021. Besides Startup India, many other central ministries/departments and state governments are promoting their own programmes towards innovation and entrepreneurship.

The government has also been supporting start-ups by providing crucial market access. Under the Digital India mission, the Government e-Marketplace (GeM) was set up. It was focussed on improving market access to start-ups, both in the industry as well as the government space. GeM has made it easier for start-ups to access the market for government consumption expenditure. It has also launched an initiative called the 'Startup

Runway', a dedicated marketplace that covers a range of sectors such as advanced manufacturing/robotics, agritech, AI and big data, AR-VR, blockchain, clean tech/renewables, consumer/home electronics, cybersecurity, edtech, health and life sciences, among others. Start-ups are now eligible for government procurement through a dedicated marketplace and have been exempted from the requirements of prior experience, prior turn over and earnest money deposit. The initiative also allows start-ups to list multiple products and services with minimal technical specifications. There is hand-holding and mentoring support to streamline the process of registration and facilitate quality improvement of products. It is this holistic approach that has borne fruit in making India one of the most vibrant start-up ecosystems in the world.

Apart from promoting start-ups, due focus has also been given on encouraging innovation and entrepreneurship at a young age. Capitalizing on the Fourth Industrial Revolution and beyond would mean we need to start training and developing our youth now. This would mean complementing the traditional education system by imparting skills crucial to innovative thinking. This is being pursued through the Atal Innovation Mission (AIM), which promotes a holistic approach towards innovation and entrepreneurship. Initiatives are targeted at all stages: ideation, deployment and scaling up. AIM has established tinkering labs (Atal Tinkering Labs, or ATLs) in schools to further curiosity, creativity, problem-solving and innovation in children from classes VI to XII. Leveraging latest technologies such as 3D printing, IoT and power tools, among others, crucial skills are being imparted to students. Today, ATLs are present across over 650 districts in India. An independent assessment of the ATLs by the Quality Council of India found that three out of four students saw their thinking broaden and felt a positive change in their personalities.

In the same vein, AIM has also been promoting incubation centres. World-class incubators have been established in universities, institutions and corporates across India. Technical support, mentorship, financial advice, funding support and market access, among others, are just some of the benefits offered to start-ups. Perhaps crucially, they create a pathway for start-ups to be ready to take on outside investment, such as from angel investors, venture capital funds and government grants, among others. Over 2,000 start-ups have benefitted from this programme since its inception. Strategic partnerships with Bill & Melinda Gates Foundation, UNDP, Marico Innovation Foundation, Freshworks, Amazon Web Services, MathWorks, GIZ and Headstart, among others, have allowed start-ups to connect with established enterprises as well.

The New Education Policy (NEP), 2020, also lays emphasis on a skills-based approach and more practical training. Early exposure to programming, coding and frontier tech such as AI-ML will ensure our young minds are at the forefront of the information age.

Apart from promoting innovation and entrepreneurship at a young age, the ecosystem protecting IPR has also been strengthened considerably. Safeguarding IP is crucial in promoting and sustaining a robust innovation ecosystem. Earlier, it used to take five years for a patent to be granted. This was too long a time. In response, the government came up with the Start-ups Intellectual Property Protection scheme, which eased the regulations for start-ups, fast-tracking the patent application process.

The entire process of granting patents, trademarks and copyrights has been re-engineered. The change has simply been massive. The granting of patents and trademarks has now been sped up to standards prevalent in developed economies such as the US and Japan. A thousand-plus staff was hired to speed up the process. Digitization of processes has no doubt played a huge role. Now, the time taken to grant a patent has been effectively reduced from five years to two years. Start-ups were also offered rebates of 80 per cent along with hand-holding support. These changes have seen the number of patents filed in India almost double between 2015 and 2021. Compared to 2015–16, when there were 12,000 patents filed, this number went up to 28,000 by 2020–21.

Trademarks, too, have seen regulatory upheaval. Earlier, the trademark rules required 74 different forms, which has now been reduced to eight. From approx. 65,000 trademarks registered in 2015–16, the number shot up to approx. 2.5 lakh in 2020–21. The number of copyrights granted rose from approx. 4,500 to approx. 16,400 during the same time period.[12]

Given the increasingly globalized world, international recognition of IP developed in India becomes important as well. India has various international arrangements in place, such as the Paris Convention and the Patent Cooperation Treaty for filing patents in a foreign country. In June 2019, India signed three additional World Intellectual Property Organization (WIPO) treaties, namely the Vienna Agreement Establishing an International Classification of the Figurative Elements of Marks, the Nice Agreement Concerning the International Classification of Goods and Services for the Purposes of the Registration of Marks and the Locarno Agreement Establishing an International Classification for Industrial Designs. These will, no doubt, help owners of IP obtain global protection for their work. Earlier, India followed its own system, which did not fully tally with international norms. By bringing international standards to India, an affirmation has been made towards protecting IP

---

[12]PIB, Ministry of Commerce and Industry, 1 August 2021, https://bit.ly/3Iin1Jn, accessed on 7 July 2022.

and innovation in India.[13] This has further affirmed the faith of foreign investors in India as well.

At the Forefront of Innovation

The most exciting aspect of watching India's start-up ecosystem evolve is seeing ground-breaking solutions being offered and developed to some of India's most pressing challenges. The innovations being designed by our young entrepreneurs have the potential to transform the economy. Home-grown entrepreneurs are now solving problems for India—problems they have seen growing up. No sector has been left untouched by their entrepreneurial zeal. In the post-1990s rush towards entrepreneurship, we see software and IT emerge as dominant sectors. However, backed by a robust digital architecture, start-ups are now changing the game in areas ranging from agriculture to finance.

Fintech has been one area where Indian start-ups are changing the rules. There has been a plethora of innovations in this space. Paytm is an early mover in the payments space that we are all familiar with. BillDesk, Razorpay, BharatPe and PhonePe are other innovators, among others, in the payments space. While we were driving the digital payments movement at NITI, I had the opportunity to interact with many of these entrepreneurs. If not for their partnership, the digital payments ecosystem would not have taken off in India. However, Indian start-ups in fintech are now moving beyond the payments space into avenues such as insurance-tech (insure-tech), digital lending and capital markets.

Take the example of Zerodha, founded by Nikhil and Nithin Kamath in 2010. The traditional business model of stock broking

[13]Saxena, Shivani, 'India Signs Three WIPO Treaties That'll Help Brand Owners with Trademarks', *BloombergQuint*, 12 June 2019, https://bit.ly/3NPhKtX, accessed on 7 July 2022.

was completely disrupted by Zerodha. Technology was an obvious differentiator, making Zerodha a more efficient platform. The discount brokerage model was pioneered by Zerodha, and focussing on the user experience ensured that they gained traction. Its biggest offering is that it has democratized wealth creation and management for individuals. Kite, another associated offering, educates investors and has played a big part in Zerodha's popularity. Today, Zerodha is among India's largest stock trading platforms, with over eight million active clients and contributes close to 15 per cent of India's retail trading volumes in markets. Another key differentiator is that Zerodha initially started with bootstrapped funding. In funding parlance, this means that the company was started without taking on an angel investor, or venture capital funding.

Cred, founded by Kunal Shah, in 2018, has been another success story. Through building a great product and clever marketing, Cred entered the unicorn club by 2021. It allows users to pay their credit card bills and earn points in return. Cred has been successful in building an ecosystem, retaining users and adding new features, such as Cred Pay, which allows user to pay rent. These are just a few examples of start-ups changing the game in financial inclusion.

Digital lending has also drawn substantial interest from entrepreneurs and investors. Lendingkart, for example, was founded in 2014 and provides loans to businesses through an online platform. KreditBee, MoneyTap and ZestMoney are some other examples of digital first lending platforms, serving markets that have traditionally been starved of credit under the traditional lending model. After digital payments, digital lending indeed seems to be the next growth avenue in India. Vast amount of data is being generated, not just through digital payments but also through the robust GST network.

Insurance is another area where start-ups are making waves. Digit is a pertinent example. It was the first unicorn of 2021 and was among the 10 largest private general insurers in just its fourth year of operations.

While fintech has been an area of strength, India's start-ups have also diversified into areas such as health, education and agriculture. 1Mg was founded in 2015 as an online platform aimed at democratizing the litany of information around medicines and lab tests. It evolved as an online marketplace for medicines and gradually began to offer diagnostic tests. In 2021, in a full display of the potential the company created, the Tata Group purchased a majority stake in the company. PharmEasy is another example. Operating in a similar space, Practo has created an online platform for people to discover and rate doctors in their vicinity, filling a huge gap in the market. Apart from a medical directory, Practo also offers facilities to book appointments online. It introduced video consultations as well, and we saw how the popularity of online consultations spiked during Covid-19. Their offerings extend to businesses as well, offering practice management software to clinics, along with health management information systems to larger clients.

Mukesh Bansal, who founded Myntra in 2007, co-founded Cure.fit in 2016. Today, under the Cure.fit platform, four products are offered to customers. Cult.fit is a chain of fitness centres. Eat.fit provides healthy food delivery options. Mind.fit provides mental health and wellness solutions. Care.fit, in turn, serves the primary healthcare market. It is fast emerging as India's premier destination for fitness and wellness. Overall, the health and wellness segment saw start-ups building solutions in areas such as remote screening and monitoring, software-aided pathology imaging, hybrid/virtual/in-person care and digital therapeutics, among others.

Another area that has seen a huge churn during Covid-19 has been education. In this context, start-ups operating in the edtech space have come to the fore. Byju's is an early example. Co-founded by Byju Raveendran and Divya Gokulnath in 2011, the learning app was launched in 2015, and within a few weeks, they had lakhs of students enrolled. In 2017, Harvard Business School published a case study on the company, particularly its impact on learning outcomes. The year 2018 saw it achieve unicorn status and by 2021, it became India's most valued start-up, ahead of Paytm. The rise has simply been phenomenal. Unacademy started from a YouTube channel in 2010, and by 2015, created an online learning platform. The vision articulated by all the founders states that through leveraging technology, the company aims to democratize education at all levels. Catering to competitive exams in India, the company allows students from far-flung areas to access top-class content and help them realize their aspirations. Without technology, they earlier lacked access to the best teachers and content. In September 2020, Unacademy achieved unicorn status, the e-learning venture after Byju's to achieve the landmark.

upGrad was launched in 2015 as an online learning platform for professionals to upskill themselves. Led by Ronnie Screwvala, Mayank Kumar, Phalgun Kompalli and Ravijot Chugh, upGrad crossed one million users in 2020. By 2021, user registrations crossed two million plus and unicorn status was achieved. We see how start-ups in similar spaces are able to carve out a niche for themselves. Vedantu, founded by Vamsi Krishna, Anand Prakash, Pulkit Jain and Saurabh Saxena in 2011, focus on live tutoring for students in classes K–12.[14] In fact, the live online classes started by the company created this category.[15]

---

[14]These grades are kindergarten (K) and the first through the twelfth grade (1–12).
[15]Kaushik, Mansvini, and Thaker, Naini, 'Meet the Players Blossoming Despite the Edtech Winter', *Forbes India*. 17 October 2022, https://bit.ly/3Uin2BZ, accessed on 20 October 2022.

Recently, the edtech sector has been facing some serious headwinds. As schools have reopened, there has been a fall in demand. However, test preparation, skilling and certification remain in demand. There is no doubt that edtech is here to stay. Entrepreneurs must seek to reinvent business models as the world returns to the pre-pandemic normal. Addressing issues such as accessibility, availability of vernacular content and reach must be the driving forces for edtech now.[16]

Apart from designing technological interventions in health and education, start-ups are also designing solutions for sectors traditionally untouched by digital technology, such as agriculture and transport.

In agriculture, start-ups are innovating, right from improving farmers' productivity to helping them get better returns for their crops. The sector has been long crying out for tech-enabled solutions, to which Indian entrepreneurs are now responding. Legacy issues include low productivity, suboptimal farm management practices, a non-existent cold chain and a lack of avenues for marketing of produce. As per estimates, more than 1,000-plus agritech start-ups have sprouted in the past few years.[17]

WayCool, for example, is building a digitally enabled supply chain, curbing the problem of wastage in produce. I have interacted with co-founder Sanjay Dasari and the other founding members several times. They first presented their model at NITI Aayog, and later, were part of a group that deliberated on the digital transformation of India's agriculture sector. They are working with thousands of farmers and supplying fresh produce to businesses.

---

[16]Ibid.

[17]Upadhyay, Harsh, and Shashank Pathak, 'The Rise of Indian Agritech Startups Since 2020: Entrackr Report', *Entrackr*, 13 July 2022, https://bit.ly/3OrDMmG, accessed on 21 July 2022.

Recently, they closed funding worth $117 million in one of the largest deals seen by an agritech start-up in India.

Ninjacart is another start-up operating in a similar space. AgNext has created a handheld device for quality grading and assaying of produce, addressing a major lacuna in the Indian market. Similarly, Intello Labs has built an AI-based imaging solution for quality grading and assaying. Licious, an online platform offering meat products, was founded in 2015. Since then, it has raised more than $300 million in funding. Wingreens Farms works with women farmers to make value-added products such as hummus, dips, sauces, etc. Recently, they closed funding to the tune of $17 million. Again, these are just a few examples.

What is more interesting is the overall trend. According to Tracxn, there exist 1,543 start-ups in this space.[18] NASSCOM, in its report, noted that agritech has been gaining considerable momentum and attracting investor interest across all stages of funding. Compared to 2020, funding to agritech start-ups saw a 437 per cent increase.

Logistics has long been a source of inefficiency in India's markets. The informal and unorganized sector was prevalent in the market. Buyers and sellers of services were rarely connected beyond their immediate geographic area. Technology has changed all of this. While the government has been investing substantially in physical infrastructure, start-ups have been leading the way in connecting businesses to service providers.

Delhivery is a well-known example, which became a unicorn in 2019. The business has evolved to providing a full suite of transport services, primarily operating in the B2B space. Shiprocket offers to automate shipping management for e-commerce companies in the B2C space. It allows business to book shipments, print labels

---

[18]'AgriTech Startups in India', Tracxn, 24 August 2022, https://bit.ly/3cAd9Pu, accessed on 21 July 2022.

and track their orders. Customers receive updates through its platform as well. Crucially, it allows e-commerce companies to pick courier services. Rivigo is employing technology to change the nature of the trucking industry. At present, drivers usually are assigned long routes of travel, spending many hours on the road. Safety is a real concern. By creating a relay model, each driver only drives a truck a certain distance, after which a new driver takes over. Technology does the job of matching, planning and assigning routes. This is a fine example of a start-up employing technology to solve a problem and improve the lives of lakhs of truck drivers and their families. Blackbuck matches businesses with owners of trucks or fleets. Through these examples, we can see how both the B2C and B2B segments of the logistics market are being digitized by start-ups. Importantly, they are also bringing with them many businesses into the formal economy, raising productivity and boosting efficiency.

The government, start-ups and corporates have also come together to develop the Unified Logistics Interface Platform (ULIP). Driven by NITI Aayog, ULIP seeks to create a multimodal logistics platform through leveraging data and technology. By integrating with other portals of transport, ULIP has the potential to bring down the cost of logistics in India.

Hyperlocal delivery, food delivery and groceries have seen substantial interest from entrepreneurs and investors alike. Zomato, with its IPO in 2021, has been leading the pack. Swiggy has also been competing in this space. Blinkit (formerly Grofers) was the first unicorn in the e-grocery space. Starting off in the grocery delivery space, it has recently pivoted to hyperlocal delivery. It has been acquired by Zomato in June 2022. Dunzo, a hyperlocal delivery service, recently raised $250 million from Reliance Retail and has been dubbed a 'soonicorn'.[19] Looking further, Dunzo will soon be using robotics and automation in its warehouses. Zepto is another new player in this space. Within just five months of starting operations, its valuation shot up to $500 million plus, after a $100 million funding round in December 2021.

What sets India's start-ups apart is that they have built technology at the core of their operations. At the same time, aware of the challenges our country faces, they have been able to devise solutions for the Indian consumer. Their market is not merely the 1.3 billion people of the country, but also the billions of people of the world who are moving from poverty to middle-class status. These volumes give them the size and scale. Flipkart introduced the cash-on-delivery model in 2010. Multiple sources have cited this as a defining moment in accelerating the adoption of e-commerce in India.[20] Now, this model is being replicated globally. India's start-ups are creating new jobs, and along with it, new models of work.

The Rise of the Gig Economy

To see young Indians have a plethora of opportunities available in terms of career choices has been one of the defining features of our economic reforms. In the immediate few years after economic reforms, we saw how new job opportunities became available. No longer were the youth bound by the 'safe' jobs of earlier times. Now, the new ecosystem in India is challenging what the very definition of a job is. Today, more and more of India's youth are being

[19]Kashyaap, Sindhu, 'Eyeing an IPO in 2-4 Years, Here's How Dunzo Aims to Grow 3X with Reliance Retail investment', *YourStory*, 19 January 2022, https://bit.ly/3PaMA17, accessed on 7 July 2022.
[20]Keshavdev, V., 'Idea of Cash on Delivery Was a Major Innovation', *Fortune India*, 8 October 2021, https://bit.ly/3OS8tm5, accessed on 7 July 2022.

attracted by the prospect of the gig economy. They are working for digital-first companies and are connected to individual 'gigs' through technology, made accessible via smartphones and cheap mobile data. Take the example of Urban Company, which now has thousands of professionals on its app, ranging from plumbers to hairdressers. Platforms such as Ola, Zomato, Swiggy, Dunzo, Zepto and Blinkit are more such examples. These platforms leverage technology to connect service providers and customers and provide a better experience for both.

This phenomenon has not necessarily been restricted to blue-collar services. Increasingly, white-collar services have also seen a movement towards the gig economy. Content writing, coding, website design, graphic design, editing and software development are just some white-collar jobs that are moving towards the gig economy. The opportunities offered by the gig economy are immense: flexibility, convenience and efficiency, to name just a few. The pandemic has accelerated the trend of workers looking for more flexibility in their employment/work.

A report released by the Boston Consulting Group stated that over the long term, the gig economy can create up to 90 million (nine crore) jobs.[21] Construction, manufacturing, retail, transport and logistics could account for the bulk of jobs created in the gig economy, the report reveals. The gig economy can create immense economic value and enhance economic opportunities, especially for low-income workers. It affords the opportunity to increase female labour force participation as well, with more flexible hours on offer. While the report acknowledges that India has always had a gig economy of sorts, it has usually existed in the informal sector. Think of seasonal agriculture labour as an

---

[21] *Unlocking the Potential of the Gig Economy in India*, Boston Consulting Group and Michael and Susan Dell Foundation, 2021, https://on.bcg.com/3PkLy3g, accessed on 18 July 2022.

example. The report identifies that what is different now is the use of technology in matching demand and supply. Technology lowers the costs for employers, while increasing demand for work. Apart from technology, I believe that this new thrust towards the gig economy is also ensuring the creation of more formal jobs—another crucial differentiator.

I believe that the gig economy will be key in defining the future of work. Recently, NITI Aayog released a report titled *India's Booming Gig and Platform Economy*.[22] The report finds that standing at 77 lakh currently, the gig economy is expected to account for 2.35 crore (23.5 million) workers by 2029–30. However, unlocking its potential in India can only be achieved through collaboration between industry and the government. Collaborating on delivering skilling programmes is one example. Platform-led skilling, akin to the Startup India movement, also emerged as a key recommendation from the report. The platform approach can create significant livelihood opportunities in areas such as mobility, hyperlocal delivery, retail and homecare. Zomato and Swiggy, for instance, have signed memorandums of understanding (MoUs) with the Ministry of Housing and Urban Affairs to impart skill among street vendors and bring them onboard.

While the gig economy delivers more flexibility to both employers and employees, structures and mechanisms have to be created to support its development in India. These could range around skilling programmes and social security, among others. The pandemic has reinforced the need for strong social security nets, and working together to develop such nets will be crucial in India's economic story going ahead. Recently, I was at the launch of Urban Company's partner stock ownership plan. A first of its

---

[22]*India's Booming Gig and Platform Economy: Perspectives and Recommendations on the Future of Work*, Policy Brief, NITI Aayog, June 2022, https://bit.ly/3uVfWbY, accessed on 18 July 2022.

kind by a company in the gig economy, it aims to award stocks worth ₹150 crore to 20,000–30,000 service partners over the next five to seven years. These are the sort of initiatives that start-ups working in the gig economy will need to take to ensure a resilient ecosystem is created.

There is a need to reduce the compliance burden to unlock the potential of the gig economy. As these are cross-cutting businesses, they have a long list of registrations and compliances. Licences are usually determined by size and granted for a year at a time. The gig economy also affords an opportunity to raise India's female labour force participation rate (LFPR), ranging between 16 per cent and 23 per cent, according to studies cited in NITI Aayog's report. This is far lower than the global average and a great source of inefficiency in the economy. Bangladesh and Vietnam, making great strides in manufacturing, have higher female LFPR, according to World Bank data.[23]

New Challenges on the Horizon

The challenges that India now faces in making its socio-economic transition are vastly different to those faced by the Four Asian Tigers, and more recently, China. The threat of climate change is very real and the report of the Working Group II in the Sixth Assessment Report (AR 6) of the Intergovernmental Panel on Climate Change (IPCC) reiterates this in no uncertain terms. Scientists have warned of a closing window in our efforts to adapt to and mitigate the effects of climate change. Furthermore, it makes clear that not only human beings but entire ecosystems are adversely impacted. Coral reefs and rainforests, among others,

---

[23]'Female labour force participation (% of labour force)-India, China, Vietnam, Bangladesh', World Development Indicators, The World Bank, https://bit.ly/3PnFEOQ, accessed on 7 July 2022.

may face irreversible damage.[24] The report also questions the level to which we will be able to adapt to climate change. Food security stands to be impacted, and consequently, India's hard-won gains in reducing poverty. The time to act is now.

At the time of writing, geopolitical tensions are riding high between Russia and the western world, following Russia's invasion of Ukraine on 24 February 2022. This comes at the back of the trade wars we have seen between the US and China, which impacted global trade. The post Second World War era of globalization, integration of global economies and supply chains may not be replicated in this new era. Covid-19 exposed the risks in concentrating supply chains in a particular geography. So, the trade environment that India sees in the years ahead will be vastly different to that seen by South Korea in the 1960s to 1990s and China from the 1980s to mid-2010s. The rise of the digital economy means that increasingly automation will have a key role to play in manufacturing. This would require a significant upskilling of workers to leverage the latest technologies.

Competitiveness will have added dimensions in this new era. Cost competitiveness, especially in manufacturing, will not just be determined by the availability of the traditional factors of production: land, labour and capital. How well enterprises can leverage technology to enhance their productivity and efficiency will also be a key determinant. Automation and AI will no doubt play important roles here. At the same time, the world is increasingly conscious of their carbon footprint. Products with a high carbon intensity are likely to see reduced demand from consumers. Countries may prescribe guidelines to which products

---

[24]Mandel, K., and J. Worland, 'The Window to Adapt to Climate Change Is "Rapidly Closing," Warns the IPCC', *Time*, 28 February 2022, https://bit.ly/3ymlgWP, accessed on 7 July 2022.

must adhere. How climate smart the production or business processes are will determine competitiveness in this new era.

Keeping these aspects in mind will be crucial for businesses and individuals going ahead. Our efforts in creating a robust digital infrastructure are already bearing fruit and much of the chapter reiterates this point. The foundations have been laid for India's private enterprise to propel India into a new era of growth and prosperity. Both the public and private sector must work together to place India at the forefront of sunrise industries. We must collectively build our capabilities to thrive in the new economy, which is digital and green.

☙

SEVEN

CLIMATE CHANGE IS EVERYONE'S BUSINESS

The biggest challenge to global prosperity and development today is climate change. According to the Intergovernmental Panel on Climate Change (IPCC), human-induced climate change is leading to more frequent and intense weather events.[1] Recent floods and hurricanes across the world are testament to this fact. The IPCC has predicted that owing to extreme climate or weather events, several ecosystems will be at risk of biodiversity loss in the near-term (2021–40). Urban areas may continue to face damage to their utilities infrastructure. Importantly, the report points out that the level to which the impact of climate change will be felt will depend on the vulnerability of the region, socio-economic development and adaptation efforts. This means that developing countries are likelier to face greater risks than the developed ones.

In the longer term (2040–2100), the hard-earned gains in reducing poverty and increasing food security all stand to be erased. While agricultural productivity has been rising over the past 50 years, the growth rate has been slowing. Extreme weather events in turn adversely impact crop production. Ocean warming will impact aquaculture. Humanitarian crises will be borne out of these climate change impacts.

The evidence is right before our eyes. According to the State of the Global Climate Report 2021, the mean temperature in 2021 was 1.11°C above the pre-industrial era (1850–1900).[2] The same report notes that the years between 2015 and 2021 have been the

[1]Pörtner, H.O., et al., (eds), 'IPCC, 2022: Summary for Policymakers', in *Climate Change 2022: Impacts, Adaptation and Vulnerability*, Contribution of Working Group II to the Sixth Assessment Report of the Intergovernmental Panel on Climate Change, Cambridge University Press, Cambridge, UK and New York, pp. 3–33, https://bit.ly/3WzmU2D, accessed on 4 November 2022.

[2]World Meteorological Organization, 'State of the Global Climate 2021', UN Environment Programme, May 2022, https://bit.ly/3t0p2Tu, accessed on 4 November, 2022

warmest years on record. Based on current policies and actions of global governments, the Climate Action Tracker (CAT) has predicted that by 2100, global temperatures will be 2.5°C–2.9°C above pre-industrial levels.[3] Even if we consider current pledges and targets, global warming will only be limited to 2.1°C by 2100. Others have predicted warming of 1.6°C if every country meets its commitments.[4] Clearly, a business-as-usual approach will not be enough.

Climate Finance, Justice and India's Leadership

Ambitious mitigation and adaptation strategies have been laid out by governments across the world, through their Nationally Determined Contributions (NDCs) as per the Paris Agreement in 2015.[5] However, meeting these NDCs require investments. Public finance would not be enough in developing countries to undertake the required adaptation and mitigation strategies. For instance, India's first NDC estimated that between 2015 and 2030, the country would need $2.5 trillion worth of investments (at 2015 prices) to finance its adaptation and mitigation strategies. For context, the size of the Indian economy was $3.1 trillion in 2021. These are mammoth investments that cannot be met from public sources of funding alone. Recognition of this investment gap has existed for some time now.

However, at the same time, it is also true that developing countries have not been responsible for the bulk of historical

[3]"Warming Projections Global Update", Climate Action Tracker, 2022, https://bit.ly/3TW6z5Q, accessed on 22 November 2022.
[4]"Getting India to Net Zero in Getting Asia to Net Zero", Asia Society Policy Institute, 2022, https://bit.ly/3sWp2Uv, accessed on 4 November 2022.
[5]The Paris Agreement requests each country to outline and communicate their post-2020 climate actions, known as their NDCs.

emissions. For instance, the US, Russia, Canada, Japan and the European Union (EU) accounted for 60 per cent of the total carbon emissions between 1751 and 2017.[6] This has left very little carbon space for the rest of the world. Consider the 1.5 degrees warming scenario. Given these historic emissions, only 14 per cent of the carbon space is left for developing countries. Continuing with the 1.5 degrees scenario, India has utilized only 1.8 per cent of the carbon space available. If the globally available carbon space is divided equitably, then India's available carbon space would have been 17.5 per cent of the total space. If we consider total CO_2 emissions (kiloton/kt), India comes up as the third-largest emitting country in the world. However, factoring in population, our country has the lowest emissions among G20 countries on a per capita basis, coming in at 1.8 metric tonnes (MT) per capita. In comparison, this figure stood at 15.2 MT per capita for Australia, 14.7 for the US, 11.7 for Russia and Korea, and 8.5 for Japan.[7] Historically, India's per capita incomes come out to be even lower.

Recognizing the need for developed nations to pay their fair share, the Copenhagen Accord of 2009 saw developed countries pledge to collectively raise $100 billion in climate finance annually till 2020. The Paris Agreement of 2015 reiterated this commitment, extending the annual flows till 2025, and setting $100 billion as the floor for the contributions of developed nations. However, since the Paris Agreement, the annual flows have averaged $74 billion a year, with 2020 seeing $83 billion worth of climate finance mobilized.[8]

---

[6]Kant, Amitabh, 'India's Leadership in the Climate Battle', Hindustan Times, 16 November 2021, https://bit.ly/3WxCFXM, accessed on 4 November 2022.
[7]World Development Indicators, World Bank, https://bit.ly/2XIV9sO, accessed on 4 November 2022.
[8]*Climate Finance Provided and Mobilised by Developed Countries in 2016–2020:*

Analysis by the Organisation for Economic Co-operation and Development (OECD), in their report, *Climate Finance Provided and Mobilised by Developed Countries in 2016–20*, shows that public finance continues to dominate, with a limited role for private capital as of now. In funds mobilized through public finance, loans tend to dominate. Mitigation sees more fund flows than adaptation efforts, with the energy and transport sectors receiving the most funding. The OECD report notes that mitigation efforts attract financing due to the size and scale of the projects on offer. A ready pipeline, along with maturing technology, is another factor. Within developing countries, the capacity to absorb loans from multilateral agencies is quite varied. Governance issues, along with domestic capital are key constraints. Given the scale of financing required, countries cannot rely on public and multilateral funds alone.

While the gap has been narrowing, a large cumulative shortfall of commitments still exists. Developed countries have not been doing enough in providing financing for climate change. These countries were able to experience socio-economic transformations during the Industrial Era. Asian countries went from being among the richest in the world to the poorest by the time World War II ended. Colonialism, no doubt, played a key role in the transfer of this wealth. Burning of fossil fuels was another key factor—a source of cheap energy and transport, and the source of plastics, among others. An era of consumerism was also ushered in with increasingly unsustainable lifestyles. A use-and-throw culture thrived. Even the Asian transformations of the past century had similar characteristics.

India has recognized that its transition cannot take the same

Insights from Disaggregated Analysis, Climate Finance and the USD 100 Billion Goal', OECD Publishing, Paris, 2020, https://bit.ly/3fxFyHw, accessed on 4 November 2022.

path seen before in the world. Considering our population and growth prospects, the demand for energy domestically is set to explode. We cannot rely on fossil fuels to burn the fires of industrialization. Rather than shy away from taking responsibility, India has emerged as a leader in the battle against climate change. In 2015, India submitted its first NDC, which pledged that 40 per cent of its electric power capacity would come from non-fossil sources by 2030. Second, India pledged to reduce the emissions intensity of GDP by 33–35 per cent compared to the 2005 levels. Finally, an additional carbon sink of 2.5–3 billion tonnes would be created through additional forest and tree cover. India not only delivered but overachieved on its commitments. Forty per cent of our power capacity came from non-fossil sources nine years ahead of schedule.

The approach taken by India is one that sees the private sector as leading these efforts, through an enabling policy environment, bolstered by diffusion of frontier technologies. At the COP26 in Glasgow in 2021, PM Modi announced India's even more ambitious climate goals, through a five-point agenda or *panchamrit*. Based on these announcements, in August 2022, India submitted its first updated NDCs. By 2030, emissions intensity of GDP would be reduced by 45 per cent of the 2005 levels, and 50 per cent electric power installed capacity would come from non-fossil sources.

Setting Benchmarks

The market for renewable energy has seen phenomenal growth in our country. In fact, among large economies, we have seen the fastest addition of renewables capacity. Between 2014 and 2021, our solar capacity increased by 18 times.[9] The REN21

---

[9]Press Information Bureau, Press Release, Ministry of New and Renewable Energy, 2021, https://bit.ly/3T8I8S2, accessed on 4 November 2022.

Renewables 2022 Global Status Report reveals that between 2014 and 2021, India's renewables market saw cumulative investments of $78.1 billion. The year 2021 alone saw $11.3 billion worth of investments.[10] These investments have seen India become the third-largest renewables market in the world, becoming globally competitive. Our country offers the second-lowest cost of solar energy at $0.035/kWh, not far behind China, at $0.034/kWh.[11] The same report notes that India offers the lowest photovoltaic (PV) project costs at $590 per kilowatt of generation capacity installed. It is private investment that has led the way. Take for instance, ReNew Power, which is now among the largest renewable energy producers in India. Relying on both wind and solar energy, ReNew has a combined capacity of 7.7 GW, with a further 5.5 GW committed. Through ReNew Green Solutions, they are enabling other companies to go green as well.

Existing players such as Tata Power are diversifying aggressively into renewable energy too. By 2027, they plan to increase the share of renewables in their generation capacity to 60 per cent, and 80 per cent by 2030. Investments worth ₹75,000 crore have been planned to meet these ambitious targets. Greenko has not only done path-breaking work on energy storage but has built one of the largest solar parks in the world. Corporate India has also been able to capitalize on the availability of green finance as well. For instance, ACME Solar, Adani Green Energy Ltd and ReNew, were all able to tap into global markets and issue green bonds.

By creating an enabling environment, India has seen investments thrive in the renewable energy space and has set a

---

[10]"Renewable 2022 Global Status Report", REN21, https://bit.ly/3UnKOw5, accessed on 4 November 2022.
[11]Hall, Max, 'Solar Power Costs Continued to Fall in 2021, Despite Rising Panel Prices', PV Magazine, 18 July 2022, https://bit.ly/3NDs89x, accessed on 4 November 2022.

precedent for other countries. We took the lead in establishing the International Solar Alliance, to which 110 countries are signatories. Domestic manufacturing of solar PV panels is being given a huge push through the PLI scheme. Initially launched with an outlay of ₹4,500 crore, the scheme aims to build domestic capabilities in solar PV manufacturing. The 2022–23 Budget announced additional outlay of ₹19,500 crore and was approved by the Cabinet in September 2022. Other key initiatives include the solar parks scheme and the rooftop solar programme.

Reducing emissions requires actions across the economy, not just in the electricity sector. The transport sector, for instance, is estimated to account for 15 per cent of energy-related CO_2 emissions in India, with the road sector alone accounting for 85 per cent of all emissions. Within roads, it is heavy-duty freight that produces the most emissions. Considering India's per capita incomes, demand for personal transport is expected to grow substantially, which, in turn, will fuel energy demand. At the same time, roads also dominate in freight, accounting for close to 65 per cent of all freight movement in India. In this context, decarbonizing our transport network is of paramount importance.

India laid out the ambitious National Electric Mobility Mission Plan (NEMMP) 2020, under which the FAME (Faster Adoption and Manufacturing of [Hybrid &] Electric Vehicles) scheme was launched to boost electric mobility in the country. Recently, tenders of electric buses (e-Buses) have been completed through the aggregation method, bringing down the total cost of ownership to levels lower than that of conventional buses. Tata Motors was awarded one of the world's largest tenders for e-Buses in July 2022. Now, there are plans to aggregate demand for up to 50,000 buses. This would enable a further reduction in costs and galvanize domestic manufacturing too. Together with FAME and the PLI scheme for automobiles and auto-components, a significant thrust has been given to electric mobility in India.

India's leading manufacturers—Hero Electric, Bajaj Auto, TVS and Hero MotoCorp—have all entered the fray. Our start-ups, too, have taken enthusiastically to the electric vehicle (EV) revolution. Newcomers such as Ola Electric and Ather Energy are jostling for market share in India's large two-wheeler market segment. These EVs offer the consumer advanced features, such as GPS navigation and low-power modes. Take for instance, Ola's Future Factory, an engineering marvel. The world's largest two-wheeler factory has the capacity to produce 20 lakh two-wheelers and is currently producing 1,000 e-scooters per day. Given that India is the world's largest market for two-wheelers and the second-largest producer of two-wheelers, the ability of the auto industry to accelerate the switch to electric will have massive ramifications for decarbonizing the road sector in the country.

In four-wheelers, Tata Motors is leading the pack, through multiple EV models already on the road. My official car is now the Tata Nexon EV, and I am thoroughly impressed with it. Mahindra, Hyundai and MG Motors have all rolled out their EVs as well, and it is expected that within the next few years, most mainstream brands will go ahead and launch their electric variants. Now that the wheels of the EV revolution have been set in motion, the transition is only a matter of time. The phenomenal growth of the e-two-wheeler segment bears strong testimony to this.

The Delhi-Meerut RRTS project, the first-of-its-kind in India, is expected to reduce travel time between the two cities to an hour, from the present three to four hours. Much of the RRTS will be powered by renewable energy. The modal share of transport, presently skewed in favour of roads, will move to public transport. This will pull cars off the road, reduce emissions and improve air quality. It is expected that 1 lakh vehicles will go off road just between Delhi and Meerut. At the same time, dedicated freight corridors (DFCs) are also being created. These will allow the movement of heavy-duty freight through faster speeds and heavy haul trains. The completion of the DFCs will reduce emissions as rail substitutes for trucks in moving freight. Cities are also being decongested through the creation of bypasses connected to expressways. The recent completion of the Eastern and Western Peripheral Expressways allows freight trucks to bypass Delhi altogether. As it can be seen, India has taken a holistic approach towards decarbonizing its transport network.

The Indian Railways, too, has set an ambitious net zero emissions target by 2030. Several cities are seeing investments in public transport through new metro projects. Regional connectivity is being boosted through the Regional Rapid Transit Systems (RRTS) projects. Alstom has successfully manufactured and delivered over a hundred electric locomotives to the Railways. This was done as part of a mammoth contract worth €3.5 billion won by Alstom back in 2015. As part of this, it is expected that 800 locomotives of 12,000 horsepower would be delivered to the Railways. These locos are capable of hauling approx. 6,000 tonnes of freight at a top speed of 120 km/hr. This will accelerate the modal shift of freight from roads, the biggest contributor of pollution in the transport sector, to railways.

The thrust towards renewable energy generation and electric mobility brings into focus energy storage, and more specifically, batteries. The PLI schemes for ACC batteries will build India's energy storage market. With an outlay of ₹18,100 crore, the selected bidders signed the Program Agreement with the Ministry of Heavy Industries in July 2022. To show the seriousness of the government, the entire process was completed in just 13 months.[12]

---

[12]"Three Companies signed Program Agreement under (PLI) Scheme for Advanced Chemistry Cell (ACC) Battery Storage', Ministry of Heavy Industries, 2022, https://bit.ly/3Ur5CCW, accessed on 4 November 2022.

Furthermore, in April 2022, NITI Aayog released the draft battery swapping policy. Battery swapping can enhance EV ownership through reducing upfront costs and the charging time associated with batteries.[13] It also reduces the need for charging infrastructure at home or at workplaces. This policy has the potential to create a robust 'battery as a service' ecosystem in India.

However, at the same time, India remains import dependent on lithium and lithium-ion batteries. To achieve self-sufficiency in battery technology, research into new technologies and recycling of existing materials are all areas that require action. Players such as Nexcharge, Okaya Power and Exicom have already taken the lead. Nexcharge has built India's automated assembly line factory of Li-ion battery packs and modules in Gujarat. Log9 Materials is working towards building batteries specifically suited to tropical conditions. They have already introduced their fast-charging and longer-duration battery packs for commercial vehicles. Lohum Cleantech is a Delhi-based start-up established in 2017, as both a manufacturer and recycler of lithium-ion batteries. Gegadyne Energy is exploring alternatives to lithium batteries and working on fast-charging technology, which can charge EV batteries in 15 minutes.

While emissions from the electricity and transport sectors have been addressed comprehensively globally, industrial emissions continue to remain a major issue. Industrial demand for fossil fuels, particularly in metals, fertilizers and cement, among others, account for close to 42 per cent of our total energy demand.[14]

---

[13]Bhatt, Amit, and Siddharth Sinha, 'Position Brief: Charting an Agenda for Battery Swapping for Two-Wheelers in India', NITI Aayog and International Council on Clean Transportation, 2022, https://bit.ly/3UopgiZ, accessed on 4 November 2022.

[14]NITI Aayog India Energy Dashboards, https://bit.ly/3sY4yLb, accessed on 4 November 2022.

Similarly, long-haul, heavy-duty trucking, shipping and aviation remain hard-to-abate sectors. Such sectors require solid or liquid fuels, and electricity cannot necessarily be used as a substitute. This is where green hydrogen comes into the picture.

Green Hydrogen to the Fore

Green hydrogen can play a crucial role in decarbonizing these hard-to-abate sectors.[15] It has been estimated that demand for green hydrogen will grow by 400 per cent by 2050, led by applications in industry and transport.[16] It will go a long way in making India energy independent as well. Currently, the bulk of the fuel for our energy requirements is imported. It has been estimated that India spends close to $160 billion annually on fuel imports. A knock-on effect of running trade deficits in energy is that the economy is vulnerable to external shocks. Take for instance the spike in energy prices after the Russia–Ukraine conflict. Oil and gas prices skyrocketed, leading to larger trade deficits and pressure on the rupee. This then creates a negative feedback loop, in which rising prices lead to a depreciating currency, raising the cost of imports.

Recognizing the vitality of green hydrogen to India's energy mix, the PM announced the National Hydrogen Mission in his Independence Day speech in 2021. If produced using our abundant solar and wind energy, green hydrogen can be the panacea for decarbonizing sectors that traditionally use oil, gas

---

[15]Kant, Amitabh, 'India's Clean Molecule Bet: At COP26, We Should Showcase Green Hydrogen as Our Best Weapon in Climate War', *The Times of India*, 28 October 2021, https://bit.ly/3h4axvb, accessed on 4 November 2022.

[16]Raj, Kowtham, et al., 'Harnessing Green Hydrogen: Opportunities for Deep Carbonisation in India', NITI Aayog and Rocky Mountain Institute, 2022, https://bit.ly/3UiqCfq, accessed on 4 November 2022.

and coal, such as steel, copper, fertilizers, cement, etc., which have been considered hard to decarbonize. Green hydrogen can play a crucial role in replacing the solid and liquid fuels used in the manufacturing processes of these industries. The good news is that neither hydrogen nor electrolyzers are new technologies. Close to 70 million tonnes of hydrogen is produced annually across the world, with India accounting for close to 8 per cent. While hydrogen produces no emissions when used, the production of hydrogen still produces carbon emissions. However, now that technologies in renewables, such as solar and wind, have matured, and robust markets created, hydrogen can be produced through clean energy, hence the term 'green hydrogen'.

India can emerge as a champion in green hydrogen by leading the way. Why India? For starters, we have one of the most significant renewable energy potentials. Pre-existing supply chains and manufacturing capabilities can push down the cost of production substantially. Combined with the availability of skilled labour in the renewables segment, India can easily position itself as the leader in green hydrogen technologies. India introduced the Green Hydrogen/Green Ammonia Policy in February 2022 as part of the National Hydrogen Mission. The policy allows for benefits such as waiver of interstate transmission charges and granting of open access to producers of green hydrogen/green ammonia. Further measures could include tax benefits and revenue recycling from carbon taxation. Establishing mandates around the usage of hydrogen or hydrogen blending can further provide a demand fillip to this nascent industry.

Working together with developed nations to establish norms for green hydrogen export can be an important avenue for India to secure export markets. India's upcoming G20 Presidency affords this opportunity. Coordinated development of standards for ships, trucks and vehicles is one example. Production of green steel is another. Iron and steel account for 7 per cent of global emissions. India accounts for 9 per cent of global steel emissions, but with a higher emission intensity of 2.5 tonne of CO_2 per tonne of crude steel against a global average of 1.8.[17] Given that India's per capita consumption of steel is still only a quarter of the global average, and that India is the second-largest producer of steel in the world, production of carbon-heavy steel would be at odds with our goals. The EU has already announced additional taxes from 2026 in iron and steel, cement, fertilizers, aluminium and electricity generation from non-EU countries that have less strict climate rules. This presents a challenge to India's goal of aligning towards global value chains. However, this is also a huge opportunity for India. The report *Harnessing Green Hydrogen: Opportunities for Deep Carbonisation in India* highlights India's potential to create the world's largest production capacity of green steel at 15–20 million tonnes by 2030.[18]

Long-distance transport is another sector in which emissions can be abated through green hydrogen. Additional demand could be created through hydrogen-derived ethanol or hydrogen fuel cells. Hydrogen could also have potential applications in the shipping and aviation sectors, too. Both are large consumers of fossil fuels. Green ammonia could be applied to produce ammonia-derived fertilizers, such as urea and diammonium phosphate. Hydrogen is also used in the production of methanol, and green hydrogen can be a potential substitute. With India's methanol economy programme underway, this sector, too, provides a source of

---

[17]Kant, Amitabh, 'How New Steel-Making Technology Can Make India Industrialise without the Need to Carbonise', *The Economic Times*, 22 July 2022, https://bit.ly/3DBPFDp, accessed on 4 November 2022.
[18]Raj, Kowtham, et al., 'Harnessing Green Hydrogen: Opportunities for Deep Carbonisation in India', NITI Aayog and Rocky Mountain Institute, 2022, https://bit.ly/3UiqCfq, accessed on 4 November 2022.

demand for green hydrogen. Based on an analysis by NITI Aayog and Rocky Mountain Institute, hydrogen demand could touch 29 million tonnes by 2050.[19] In the near term, refining and ammonia can be the key drivers of demand. Steel and long-haul trucking hold much potential in the long term.

It has been encouraging to see India Inc. take up this challenge with enthusiasm. Reliance Industries, for instance, has planned investments in green hydrogen as part of their ₹75,000 crore renewable energy push. Already a large producer of grey hydrogen, Reliance plans on transitioning to producing green hydrogen by 2025. Larsen & Toubro (L&T) and ReNew Power have joined hands to tap India's green hydrogen market. Total Energies and the Adani Group have come together to develop an ecosystem around green hydrogen, in a deal worth up to $50 billion over 10 years. This would see them produce 1 million metric tonnes per annum (mmta) of green hydrogen by 2030. The ACME Group has also set up the world's first integrated pilot project for green hydrogen and green ammonia plant at Bikaner in Rajasthan. This would be the first green hydrogen plant in India, powered by 5 MW of solar panels, which can be expanded up to 10 MW. The ACME group has accelerated its quest for green hydrogen and green ammonia, announcing investments of ₹1.5 trillion on three projects in Tamil Nadu, Karnataka and also Oman. The Greenko Group is now moving towards green hydrogen and ammonia as well. Together with ONGC, the group plans to invest over $6 billion in producing green ammonia and other green hydrogen derivatives in India. The Sajjan Jindal-led JSW Steel has also been exploring the use of green steel, while JSW Energy has been exploring the production of green hydrogen, leveraging global partnerships.

---

[19]Ibid.

However, before green hydrogen becomes a reality, there is much work to be done. Power costs, including generation and transmission, account for close to 70–75 per cent of the total green hydrogen cost. To make India's green hydrogen industry globally competitive, we must seek to bring the cost of renewables down to ₹1 Kw/h. At the same time, domestic R&D will be of crucial importance. India Inc. must focus on bringing down the cost of electrolyzers and ensure self-reliance in its production. Combined with a fall in the price of renewable energy and a fall in the cost of electrolyzers, the price of green hydrogen could come down to $0.6–1.2/kg, according to the analysis by NITI Aayog and the Rocky Mountain Institute.

India is climatically blessed, has top-class entrepreneurship and the unique opportunity to emerge as the global production and export hub of green hydrogen, as well as the electrolyser manufacturer of the world.

Circular Economy Takes Centre Stage

India sees the fight against climate change as a collective one, with individual action at the core. Notably, India's updated NDCs also include a statement on propagating a healthy and sustainable lifestyle, titled LiFE (Lifestyle for Environment).

In October 2022, in the presence of the United Nations Secretary General, the PM launched the LiFE global movement. The movement is a testament to the rising urgency around climate change. Large-scale climate action to nudge behaviour change and encourage daily sustainable habits can have a tremendous impact. It is a clarion call to each person to take the responsibility of becoming trustees of the environment. LiFE draws on practices that are deeply ingrained in Indian lifestyle. Just like with yoga, which has become part of global lifestyles, LiFE can nudge individuals towards climate-friendly lifestyles.

The launch of LiFE brings to the centre stage the potential of the circular economy in mitigating and adapting to climate change. Circular supply chains, recovery and recycling, product life extension, sharing platforms, and product as a service are just some of the emerging business models. Indian start-ups and corporates are innovating across each of these new models.

According to a report by Kalaari Capital, the circular economy is still in its nascent stage in India, attracting some $1.8 billion worth of funding over the past five years. The highest value investments are made in the energy and transport sector. However, they still see huge opportunities for start-ups to thrive in areas such fashion, food systems, mobility, construction and rare-earth metals.[20] Convenience, cost and consciousness are the three key pillars to mainstream circular economy adoption, according to the report. Circular economy solutions must be made as convenient as the linear (traditional) economy. Second, the cost of such products and services must be brought down to levels seen in the linear economy. Otherwise, consumer adoption may be limited. Third, consciousness remains an untapped market. Consumers are more likely to consider convenience and cost before environmental considerations of products. For start-ups in this space, devising solutions that address all three would be key to their success.

The range of areas in which our entrepreneurs are innovating is astonishing. Take for instance Nexus Power, which is making rechargeable, bio-organic and bio-degradable EV batteries utilizing crop residue. Attero Recycling, involved in the recycling of lithium-ion batteries, has invested $1 billion towards the development of global recycling facilities. This technology, developed in India and patented globally, can recycle materials with efficiency, retaining

[20]*Circular Economy: A Kalaari Capital Report,* 2022, https://bit.ly/3NzVTrO, accessed on 4 November 2022.

their purity. Banyan Nation is recycling plastics and training informal workers. The Kanpur-based Phool.Co is solving the problem of floral waste by turning it into organic fertilizer and incense sticks. By employing rural women self-help groups, they are also able to raise India's female labour force participation. Graviky Labs is turning air pollution into ink. They recently partnered with fashion labels to print apparel and are looking at developing technology that will enable the creation of plastics and fuels from captured CO_2.

Given the water stress India faces, Indra Water, founded in 2018, seeks to treat and reuse wastewater. Their technology seems promising. From among 236 contestants across 38 countries, they won the urban water challenge at the Stockholm World Water Week 2019. Carbon Craft Design is turning used tyres and other waste carbon into tiles for homes. Interestingly, they incorporate a 200-year craft, which combines this carbon with marble chips, marble powder and cement to produce tiles. These are but a few examples. What this tells us is that India's entrepreneurs are willing to dive into unconventional areas and unlock value in not just an economic sense but also socially.

Food systems are likely to come under increasing stress as climate change can reduce yields, increase wastage, damage crops and lead to crop failures, among others. This is another area where urgent action is required. Again, India's entrepreneurs have come to the fore. Ninjacart and WayCool are solving problems across supply chains, leading to lesser wastage and better market access for farmers. On the input side, DeHaat, Cropin and BharatAgri are advising farmers on ways to improve resource efficiency and improve productivity. At the same time, start-ups are also promoting a healthier lifestyle through the introduction of nutritious products made from traditional grains, such as millets. Slurrp Farm is making snacks for kids using millets, such as ragi and jowar. Considering 2023 has been declared the International Year of Millets by the UN, initiatives such as these are key in raising demand for traditional grains. In turn, these are water-efficient, contributing to our water security. The future is indeed exciting in the circular economy space. Indian entrepreneurs are poised to deliver on new business models that will bring to the fore the circular economy.

Pathways to Net Zero by 2050

Even before announcing updated targets, India was one of the few countries on track to meet their NDCs. Notably, many developed countries, responsible for historic emissions, fell behind the curve in terms of climate action. For instance, the US dropping out of the Paris Agreement and then rejoining, is one example. The insufficient flow of climate finance, is another. However, as the Climate Action Tracker has shown, more ambitious action is needed to limit global warming to well below 2°C and the goal of 1.5°C by 2100 as per the Paris Agreement. India has already announced an ambitious strategy of net zero emissions by 2070. In the 2070 net-zero scenario, India can achieve a 48 per cent reduction in carbon intensity of GDP by 2030, against a target of 45 per cent; reduce carbon emissions by 1.9 billion tonnes, against a target of 1 billion; and increase the share of renewables in installed capacity to 60 per cent, against a target of 50 per cent.[21] Clearly, we are on track to overshoot our targets by 2030.

As the economy stabilizes, the coming years present a case for India to be even more ambitious and aim to go net zero by 2050. The potential paths India can take presents interesting policy implications. An analysis by the Asia Society Policy Institute

---

[21]'Getting India to Net Zero', Asia Society Policy Institute, 26 August 2022, https://bit.ly/3UmISEc, accessed on 4 November 2022.

shows that a net zero 2050 goal could boost GDP by 7.3 per cent and create 20 million additional jobs by 2032.[22] By pursuing this target, we would achieve a reduction in carbon intensity of 73 per cent by 2030, achieve reduction of 6.8 billion tonnes of carbon emissions, and increase share of renewables in capacity to 81 per cent.

On the policy front, introducing carbon pricing, supporting renewables and EV industries, biofuel and green hydrogen mandates, along with revenue recycling are potential policy options. Phasing down coal-based power in a calibrated manner has been India's approach. As we are currently in the early phase of our development, India cannot simply substitute renewable and fossil fuel-based power. The standards to which India is held cannot be the same as the developed countries of today, who have been responsible for most of the cumulative emissions so far. The transition period envisages that India can continue to meet its climate targets, whilst ensuring access to all.

At the same time, state governments must take the lead in ensuring the financial health of their ailing distribution companies (DISCOMs). To this end, the Ministry of Power launched the Revamped Distribution Sector Scheme in June 2022, with an outlay of ₹3 lakh crore between 2022 and 2026. This scheme incentivizes strengthening of the distribution infrastructure, which will have the effect of reducing transmission and distribution losses and lowering the gap between costs and revenues.

Technologies such as green hydrogen, green metals, carbon capture and storage, next-generation batteries, heat pumps and next-generation solar PV would be critical to reach global climate targets. Investments in these futuristic technologies can unlock massive growth opportunities. The government can incentivize such

---

[22]Ibid.

investments by the private sector through technology mandates and by emerging as a buyer of advanced technology. We have already shown the way with the Ujala scheme, bringing down the cost of LEDs, and we can do the same in emerging solar and battery technologies.

The gains in GDP largely accrue from increased investments and improving balance of trade. The Asia Society Policy Institute estimates that India would need cumulative investments of $10 trillion from the baseline (2021) to reach net zero by 2070.[23]Reaching net zero by 2050 would require an additional $3.7 trillion of investments. Clearly, India cannot rely on public sources of funding alone. Private investment will have to be leveraged, along with the commitments made by developed countries as per the Paris Agreement. India has noted that its NDCs are dependent on the availability of $1 trillion of climate finance.

There is much that can be done to reform the global green finance system as well. Private finance still forms a small share of total climate finance. One reason cited by the OECD for low uptake of private or blended finance in developing countries was the high perceived investment risks. Concern around capacity, a pipeline of investible projects and policy uncertainty are some examples. For instance, India has been able to attract private investments in the renewable energy space through a favourable policy environment.

The *Report of the G20 Eminent Persons Group on Global Financial Governance* provides some recommendations. It calls for leveraging international financial institutions (IFIs) to help reduce and manage risk in developing countries. Shifting the business model of these IFIs towards risk mitigation, rather than direct lending, could help mobilize private capital flows. Providing credit

---

[23]'Getting India to Net Zero in Getting Asia to Net Zero', Asia Society Policy Institute, 2022, https://bit.ly/3sWp2Uv, accessed on 4 November 2022.

enhancement services, along with technical support to developing countries, can form the foundations of the new business model. Blended finance and first-loss guarantees are other avenues through which funding for climate investments can be scaled up. Such moves would be crucial to attracting private capital. The global system could effectively leverage the expertise of the Multilateral Investment Guarantee Agency. Together, they can standardize processes and contracts as well as crowd-in private reinsurers.

At the same time, capacities must be built in developing countries to create pipelines of projects with a scale and diversification level that would attract institutional investors. Securitization of several related projects, along with green bonds and funds, could draw in institutional investors. There are lessons here for India, too. With a pipeline of investible projects, along with strong institutional capacity through governance reforms, India is well placed to attract global capital.

Apart from building these capabilities, monetary policy also has an important role to play in supporting green finance in India. This can range from micro and macro prudential tools, to market development and financial governance-based initiatives.[24] Analysis of data released by the RBI reveals that bank lending to renewable energy projects constituted 7.9 per cent of the outstanding bank credit to the power-generation sector in March 2020, up from 5.4 per cent in March 2015.[25] The 21st Report of the Standing Committee on Energy, published in February 2022, contained some recommendations. Setting up of Infrastructure Development Funds (IDFs), infrastructure investment trusts

[24]Mehta, Charmi, 'Re-Imagining Climate Finance', ORF Issue Brief No. 575, Observer Research Foundation, https://bit.ly/3fx1JO6, accessed on 4 November 2022.
[25]'Database on Indian Economy', Reserve Bank of India, https://bit.ly/3UZqYbs, accessed on 22 November 2022.

(InvITs), alternate investment funds, green bonds and masala bonds were some ideas. The committee also recommended that the Ministry of Finance and the RBI explore Renewable Finance Obligations for commercial banks. Since bank lending constitutes the bulk of credit in India, it is essential that bank balance sheets are made resilient to climate change. Charmi Mehta cites a survey of Indian banks which reveals that as of early 2022, none of the 34 scheduled commercial banks assessed the resilience of their portfolios.[26] Building in environmental, social and governance (ESG) considerations in lending norms is another avenue for action. A similar recommendation was made by the G20 Eminent Persons Group, which called for a new set of prudential norms for multilateral development banks.

The World's Tech Garage

A distinctive advantage available to India is a vast pool of human capital, especially young engineers and data-hungry entrepreneurs. There is absolutely no doubt that India is fast emerging as the tech garage of the world. The investments in both the tech and cleantech space have witnessed a massive growth, and this trend is likely to continue.

However, to sustain this momentum, it is important for India to explore new technologies that can power India's climate ambitions and provide the much-needed boost to cleantech solutions. This requires dedicated investments and R&D into new technological avenues. On the battery storage front, we must explore sodium ion batteries, redox flow batteries, nanowire batteries and new-generation lithium-ion batteries such as lithium–sulphur and

---

[26]Mehta, Charmi, 'Re-Imagining Climate Finance', ORF Issue Brief No. 575, Observer Research Foundation, https://bit.ly/3fx1JO6, accessed on 4 November 2022.

lithium metal, among others. Lithium–sulphur batteries, for instance, can have applications in aviation and space, owing to their high densities. Similarly, solid state batteries are more energy dense, have faster charging and a longer shelf life, and provide higher range.

On the solar front, we must strive to explore recently commercialized technologies that are gaining traction in India and also other parts of the world. These include technologies such as bifacial solar panels, where energy is generated from both the top and bottom of solar panels, heterojunction, solar trackers and kerfless solar wafer. In the long term, tandem module solar cells and perovskite solar cells also need to be explored and mainstreamed. For our ambitions in green hydrogen to witness resounding success, cracking electrolyzer technology is a must. Many companies, such as Siemens and Ohmium, are working on ushering next-generation PEM technologies. Companies such as Bloom Energy and Topsoe (formerly Haldor Topsøe) are trying to work on solid oxide electrolyzers. Therefore, in the long run, our success in cleantech depends on investments in sunrise areas of growth. These should be across a range of areas, be it renewables, such as solar and wind or biofuels. Solar and green hydrogen-based production of green metals and using highly durable electrolyzers for green hydrogen are just some of the numerous avenues that can accelerate India's technical prowess in combatting climate change.

India Inc.: Going Digital, Going Green

As has been the case in India's economic transformation over the past three decades, it is the private sector that must lead the way in the next transition to come. Globally, we are seeing a movement towards low-carbon products and India itself is spearheading the movement on sustainable lifestyles, through LiFE. The carbon tariffs set to be issued by the EU are just the first of such taxes that may come up. High-carbon products will no longer be competitive. Globally investors are increasingly looking at ESG considerations. Financial institutions are looking to de-risk their balance sheets by scaling down funding for carbon-heavy products. The writing is on the wall. What defined competitiveness in the era of growth seen by the West, East and Southeast Asia will no longer hold relevance. India Inc. must strive to get ahead of the curve in terms of piloting and scaling technologies. Increasing corporate R&D is a must. The government stands committed to creating an enabling policy environment. With the help of policy support, India has managed to build a globally competitive renewable energy market. Policy initiatives have been taken in areas such as green hydrogen and ACC batteries. It is up to the private sector to innovate, scale and bring these technologies to the market. We must look at the future of competitiveness, not the past. India Inc. must go digital, and they must go green.

Many Indian companies have already announced ambitious strategies to this end. Infosys stands out in this context. It achieved carbon neutrality in 2020, 30 years ahead of schedule.[27] At the same time, it announced its ESG Vision 2030 to remain at the forefront of climate change. Wipro has committed to achieving net-zero emissions by 2040, and a 55 per cent reduction in emissions by 2030, from a base of 2016–17. Reliance Industries has announced plans to go net zero by 2035. Tata Consultancy Services and Indian Railways plan to go net zero by 2030 and HDFC by 2032. Sixty-four Indian companies have committed towards the Science Based Targets initiative, a partnership between

---

[27]'Infosys Turns Carbon Neutral 30 Years Ahead of 2050, the Timeline Set by the Paris Agreement', Press Release, Infosys, 28 October 2020, https://infy. com/3AAciaA, accessed on 22 November 2022.

the Carbon Disclosure Project, UN Global Compact, the World Resources Institute and the World Wildlife Fund, which aims to catalyse climate action through the private sector. Of these 64 companies, 37 have committed towards net-zero targets. These include Ambuja Cement, ACC Ltd, Hindalco, Hindustan Zinc, Flipkart, Bharti Airtel and Mahindra & Mahindra, among others. Vedanta, led by Anil Agarwal, is successfully making the transition into digital technologies, such as semi-conductors. I applaud him for showing the vision to transition from minerals to digital technologies. This will go a long way towards building up India's capability in the semiconductor space.

The ambitious targets set by India Inc., combined with the innovative capability of our start-ups and entrepreneurs, will place India at the forefront of this fight against climate change. We will have to chart a new course and model of development. We have all the ingredients in place. Now is the time to act.

⌒∽⌒

EPILOGUE

BEYOND INDIA@75

We have indeed come a long way since the days post-Independence. From severely lacking in technology, infrastructure and human capital, India is now poised to become a world leader in these fields. Private enterprise has moved from the peripheries to play a leading role in India's development story. Today's youth no longer want the safety of jobs. They are venturing out and building businesses and solutions around India's most intractable problems. Indian entrepreneurs, business leaders and innovators are now being recognized on the global stage. From an inefficient, uninventive and rent-seeking economy, India is now emerging as an efficient, innovative and dynamic economy.

India's increasingly maturing innovation ecosystem has led to a substantial improvement in the Global Innovation Index (GII), published by WIPO since 2007. In 2021, India ranked forty-sixth on the GII, a substantial improvement from eighty-first in 2015. The efforts of scientific departments such as the Department of Atomic Energy, the Ministry of Science and Technology, and the Department of Space, along with AIM and the Department for Promotion of Industry and Internal Trade, in building an innovation ecosystem and a robust digital architecture have no doubt played a major role in this improvement and further developing India's innovation ecosystem.

A robust innovation ecosystem means that India has the potential to become a 'tech garage' of the world.[1] We have all the necessary ingredients to develop innovative, tech-enabled solutions across sectors such as agriculture, education, health, water and financial inclusion. India presents several use case scenarios for emerging technologies, and solutions that have been developed and scaled in India can easily be replicated across the country,

[1]Kant, Amitabh, 'India Can Soon Be the Tech Garage of the World', *Mint*, 9 September 2020, https://bit.ly/3RNPZFs, accessed on 19 July 2022.

given the considerable size of our markets. NITI Aayog has been working closely with entrepreneurs, industry leaders and academics to devise technological solutions for India's long-standing issues through the Technology Commons network. Take the example of ULIP, which recently found mention in the finance minister's Budget Speech of 2022.[2] This product, developed by entrepreneurs and industry leaders brought together by NITI Aayog, will enable the creation of a more efficient logistics network, boosting our competitiveness.

Our robust digital infrastructure, backed by a maturing innovation ecosystem, has the potential to help India leapfrog into a new technological era. Many opportunities have been afforded by frontier technologies. However, the path must still be traversed and it will be full of new challenges. It is only through PPPs that we will achieve our goals.

India's Aspirations

There are many lessons to be learnt from India's past as it enters the next phase of its industrial journey. India commanded 24 per cent of the global GDP at the eve of colonization. In purchasing power parity terms, India's per capita income stood at $1,162 in 1700, against a world average of $1,746.[3] Comparing incomes using purchasing power parities gives a better picture of the prevalent standards of living in the country. By the time of Independence, our share in the global GDP had fallen to approx. 5 per cent. Our

---

[2]Budget 2022–2023: Speech of Nirmala Sitharaman, Minister of Finance, Government of India, 1 February 2022, budget_speech.pdf (indiabudget.gov. in), accessed on 19 July 2022.

[3]Maddison Project Database 2020, Bolt, Jutta, and Jan Luiten van Zanden, 'Maddison Style Estimates of the Evolution of the World Economy. A New 2020 Update', Groningen Growth and Development Centre, https://bit.ly/3PbmyL7, accessed on 8 July 2022.

per capita income had fallen to $985, while the global average had risen to $4,674. The impact of colonialism was clear. In the years following Independence, the Licence Raj reigned supreme. Private enterprise was shackled and the government was at the commanding heights of the economy. Between 1947 and 1990, our incomes roughly doubled to levels of $2,000. With the economic reforms of the 1990s, income began to accelerate, going from approx. $2,000 to approx. $6,500 between 1990 and 2020. In 30 years, incomes trebled.

Despite exhibiting impressive growth since the 1990s, India still lags behind countries that were once peers: Japan, South Korea, China and Taiwan. Income in South Korea reached $13,900 by 1990, and in 2020, touched $40,000. China saw growth accelerating in the 1980s, when its per capita income was $1,900. By 2010, income reached $9,600 and by 2020, it had reached $14,000. In terms of sheer size, the Indian economy reached a size of $3 trillion (in real terms), while the size of the Korean economy stood at $1.6 trillion in 2020.

However, per capita income and purchasing power matter more than the size of the economy. Consider how far India has fallen. We were at similar levels to Korea and China in 1947. Now, 75 years later, income in Korea is seven times that of India and that of China is 2.6 times that of India. If we don't account for purchasing power differences, then income in Korea is 16 times that of India and that of China is five times. This reflects the importance of economic growth.

Joe Studwell provides a fascinating account in his book about what went right in these growth stories.[4] Rising agricultural productivity, directing investments towards manufacturing and effective financial intermediation were the key ingredients in

---

[4]Studwell, Joe, *How Asia Works: Success and Failure in the World's Most Dynamic Region,* Profile Books, London, 2013.

the success of these nations. A pool of domestic savings was leveraged effectively by directing these investments to intensive, small-scale agriculture and manufacturing activities. Building the capabilities of private enterprise to be globally competitive was a crucial aspect in this strategy. Studwell calls this 'export discipline'. By conditioning domestic incentives to export targets, globally competitive firms were created. Firms that missed targets did not have the luxury of domestic protection through incentives and tariffs. This ensured that only the most productive and efficient firms survived.

India will need to create similar domestic champions that will thrive on the global stage. This is an important differentiator between the success stories of Japan, Korea and China, as against the experiences of Indonesia, Malaysia and Thailand. While foreign investment and technology played a key role in East Asia, countries in Southeast Asia were unable to develop strong domestic brands and capabilities. Consequently, these countries remained at the lower end of value addition in GVCs.

At present, India is classified as a lower-middle income country. We are at half the income of the lowest upper-middle income country and at one-sixth the income of the lowest high-income country. Our aspiration to become a high-income country at 100 years of Independence in 2047 will only be met through sustained growth. First, let us see where we are currently:

Table 2: Comparing India and Asia in 2021

Size of Economy	India	China	Korea
Current, $ trillion (trn)	3.2	17.7	1.8
Real, $ trn[5]	2.7	15.8	1.7

[5]Constant (2015) US dollars. Source: The World Bank. Estimated values for 2021.

Real PPP, \$ trn[6]	9.3	24.9	2.3
Per Capita Incomes	**India**	**China**	**Korea**
Current, \$	\$2,100	\$10,434	\$31,631
Real, \$	\$1,961	\$11,118	\$32,645
Real PPP, \$	\$6,675	\$17,603	\$44,116

Source: World Development Indicators, The World Bank.

The World Bank defines countries using thresholds based on current per capita incomes.[7] Table 3 gives the classifications.

Table 3: Current World Bank Income Classifications in 2022

Classification	Threshold
Low Income	< \$1,045
Lower Middle	\$1,046 – \$4,095
Upper Middle	\$4,096 – \$12,695
High Income	> \$12,696

Source: World Bank Country and Lending Groups, The World Bank, https://bit.ly/3DDWDJj, accessed on 27 October 2022.

Growth will be the only way to sustain India's socio-economic transition. Let us consider some basic scenarios to illustrate the

---

[6]Constant (2017) PPP dollars. Source: The World Bank. Estimated values for 2021.

[7]The World Bank uses Gross National Income (GNI) to define thresholds. GNI includes GDP and income earned by residents from abroad. Both GDP per capita and GNI per capita are closely correlated. In India's case, GDP per capita has been slightly greater (approx. 1 per cent) than GNI, owing to our current account deficit. The World Bank revises these thresholds annually to account for inflation.

power of compounding. A growth rate of 6 per cent during 2022–47 will see the Indian economy reach a size of $16.4 trillion in real terms by 2047.[8] A growth rate of 8 per cent in this period will see the economy reach a size of $20.6 trillion. A 10 per cent growth for the next 25 years will see the economy reach a size of $32.6 trillion by 2047. This is the power of compounding. A 6 per cent real growth rate would translate into per capita income of $10,000 by 2047. An 8 per cent growth rate would see per capita income touch $14,000 and a 10 per cent growth rate would see income touch $22,000. Again, the power of compounding is there to see.

As is evident, India is likely to be stuck in a middle-income trap in the low-baseline growth scenarios. It is only through sustained growth will we see India transformed. To achieve that, our investment and saving rates will need to increase from approx. 29–30 per cent of GDP to approx. 35 per cent of GDP in the high-growth scenarios.

Future Avenues of Growth

Data will be central to our future growth aspirations. India will have to go from being a data-rich country to being a data-intelligent country. Since undertaking a drive towards digitization, we have been generating vast amounts of data. For instance, in September 2022, 680 crore (6.8 billion) transactions took place on UPI—an average of 22 crore (220 million) transactions daily. The GST network has generated approx. 303 crore e-way bills and 1,580 crore-plus invoices have been uploaded on the portal as of February 2022. The data being generated through these transactions contain crucial information, and, if analysed, can reveal much about the financial health of an individual or a company.

---

[8]Assuming a constant inflation rate differential between the USD and INR. This would imply a constant exchange rate.

The National Digital Health Mission will facilitate technology-enabled healthcare. Through a unique health ID, medical history can be stored and retrieved as needed. While the initiative is underway, the data it will generate will be massive. Apart from individuals, all doctors, medical facilities, labs and hospitals will also be given a unique ID. Initiatives such as eNAM, Soil Health Card, Kisan Credit Card and Pradhan Mantri Fasal Bima Yojana (crop insurance) have been generating vast amounts of granular data, often at the farmer or plot level.

These datasets, along with a steadily expanding digital footprint, will be key to developing AI-ML-based solutions across sectors of the economy such as water, agriculture, health and education, among others. Already, we see AI solutions championed by start-ups being deployed across the spectrum. From predicting machine failures to providing real-time manufacturing insights, these solutions are paving the way for industries to become lean and tech-driven. And this would, in turn, allow our industries to become globally competitive. If we are able to innovate in these areas, then there is no reason why the success seen in India cannot be replicated in other developing countries. India must strive to show the world the way in the responsible use of technology and leverage technology for public good.

The success of the JAM Trinity and digital payments means that India has made significant strides in ensuring financial inclusion. However, much remains to be done in making financial instruments such as credit and insurance widely available. This is where the recently unveiled Account Aggregator (AA) network would come in. The AA network would enable the sharing of financial records, securely and with full, informed consent of individuals or businesses. Let me illustrate with an example. An individual applying for a loan gives consent to an AA to access their financial information, say in the form of bank statements.

The financial information put together by the AA can then be used by the prospective lender to evaluate the credit worthiness of the individual or business. Information, rather than collateral, will drive the lending process now. This has the potential to greatly expand access to individuals and businesses that may be excluded from credit markets based on old lending models.

Privacy and security have been built into the AA framework. It draws on the consent mechanism, designed by the principles of Data Empowerment and Protection Architecture, a policy proposed by NITI Aayog. End-to-end encryption ensures security of data. Perhaps most importantly, AAs are not permitted to store, process or sell data. This differentiates them from modern tech behemoths, where monetizing consumer data is at the core of their business models.

At present, many major banks have joined the network. However, data from other information providers, such as GST, income tax, insurance, NBFCs, pensions, provident fund, etc., are yet to be made available. This remains a focus area for the government. The creation of the AA framework produces immense opportunities for private enterprise to take forward the agenda of financial inclusion to its natural conclusion. With AAs generating vast amounts of data, opportunities to analyse this data exist, leveraging the latest technologies such as AI-ML and data analytics.

Along with AAs, the time has probably come for India to have its first digital bank. These digital banks hold the promise of overcoming the persistent policy challenge of credit deepening. The traditional challenges have been information asymmetry and the costs involved, which raises the minimum ticket size of loans and cost of loans. Many of our 6.4 crore plus MSMEs exist in the trading and retail space, and do not have any collateral to offer per se. The NBFCs have been filling this gap, but since they cannot collect deposits, they raise funds from money markets, which are often more volatile and costlier. The Trade Receivables Discounting System platform has also found limited takers. So, there exists a real credit constraint in the economy, and technology can help solve this.

A full-stack digital bank would function in the same way as a physical one. It would collect deposits, issue loans and cards. It can leverage advanced technologies to issue credit lines and loans to borrowers. The discussion paper on licencing and regulatory regime for digital banks released by NITI Aayog discusses the policy issues involved. Given the strides India has made in financial inclusion, a full-stack digital bank is not far from reality.

Apart from a revolution in finance, we are at the cusp of a mobility revolution as well. Mobility will now be shared, connected and clean. We have already seen the advent of the shared economy in mobility through the arrival of Uber and Ola, which harnessed the app-based digital revolution seen in India. There is no doubt in my mind that they have forever altered the way we travel within cities.

Electric mobility is now the next avenue we must conquer. I have personally driven the electric vehicle (EV) movement in India and firmly believe that the companies that go electric will flourish. I have also proposed that the government should procure only EVs, as the total cost of ownership is cheaper. Tata Nexon EV has replaced Maruti Ciaz as my official vehicle. Mahindra has unveiled five electric concept cars that are underpinned by INGLO EV skateboard architecture. The five all-new electric SUVs signify an Indian auto company's major initiative to step into the global EV arena. It has announced plans to set up a dedicated EV manufacturing facility in Pune. I firmly believe that Maruti should also accelerate the pace of transformation and go electric.

Rapid innovations in the battery technology space have led to prices falling considerably. For instance, the price of lithium-ion batteries has fallen by more than 90 per cent in the past decade.

As battery prices continue to fall, soon the costs will be at par with traditional internal combustion engines (ICE or IC engine). Globally, this is driving the electric mobility revolution. The government has been leading the way in notifying the FAME I and FAME II schemes. Several states have also notified their own EV policies.

As a result of these initiatives, we are definitely seeing increased EV adoption in India. The sales of EVs in calendar year 2021 were approx. 3 lakh, compared to approx. 1.2 lakh in 2020. Monthly sales data reveals a steady acceleration in EV adoption. In December 2021, 50,000 units were sold, compared to an average of 15,000 units a month in 2020. By August 2022, this number increased to 87,038 units a month. What has changed? The remodelled FAME II policy has played an important role in raising demand. The new scheme increased the subsidy for electric two-wheelers by 50 per cent, and an aggregation strategy was adopted for electric three-wheelers and electric-buses (e-Bus). e-Buses were proposed for cities with a population of over one million. Initially, Kolkata, Delhi, Bengaluru, Hyderabad and Surat utilized the new model. A tender has been rolled out for these five cities to procure a combined 5,450 e-Buses, the largest global tender for e-Buses to date. The prices discovered were among the lowest ever, and extremely close to the operational cost of diesel buses.

With rising incomes, demand for electronic products, cars and two-wheelers is expected to rise. Battery storage promises to be a crucial tool in our goal towards achieving sustainable development. Manufacturing of advanced batteries has the potential to be one of the largest economic opportunities of the twenty-first century, not just for India but also globally. To this end, in May 2021, the government approved the PLI scheme for manufacturing ACC batteries at an estimated outlay of ˋ18,100 crore over five years from the date of manufacturing. The scheme envisages setting up of a cumulative manufacturing capacity of 50 GWh for ACCs and an additional cumulative capacity of 5 GWh for niche ACC technologies.

Substantial policy thrust has been given towards the electric mobility revolution. Through enabling policies, private enterprises are innovating to develop globally competitive products. This is a fine example of how the government sees future industries evolving in the country. The government creates an enabling environment through proactive policy, while the private sector is left to innovate and create world-class products.

Renewable energy is another high-priority area. Solar, wind and hydro energy also form a significant part of India's energy mix. Our cumulative target stands at generating 500 GW of energy through renewable sources. As with ACC batteries, the GoI launched a PLI scheme for the manufacture of solar photovoltaic (PV) modules to boost domestic manufacturing capabilities and to reduce import dependence. Apart from solar energy, India also has the potential to industrialize without the need to 'carbonize' through green hydrogen. Research and development will be crucial to the development of India's green hydrogen capabilities, and this is where the industry, start-ups and entrepreneurs must play leading roles.

Electronic goods will remain an area with high potential, especially with rising incomes and new innovations. In this context, semiconductor and display manufacturing will bring massive growth opportunities for private enterprise and the nation. The proliferation of connected devices and the potential of IoT mean that demand is only going to go up. To boost the competitiveness of India's manufacturing, a PLI scheme, with an outlay of ₹76,000 crore (approx. $10 billion) has been launched. Production incentives are available across the value chain. This scheme aims to nurture 20 domestic companies in semiconductor design and aims to help them achieve a turnover of ₹1,500 crore within five years.[9]

To drive long-term competitiveness, India Semiconductor Mission has also been set up. This scheme comes at an opportune time, when the world is reeling under a semiconductor shortage, which is impacting not just electronics manufacturing but also auto manufacturing, among others. Again, we see the government committing towards developing private-sector capabilities, unlike going at it alone, as it had done in the post-Independence era. These interventions are expected to not only give the consumer electronics market a huge fillip, but they also have the potential to create exciting new opportunities in IoT and smart mobility, among others.

Another sector that has recently been liberalized by the government is geospatial systems, which play a crucial role in data visualization and in informing decision-making across key sectors such as infrastructure, industry, water and agriculture, among others. Recognizing the importance, the PM has championed reforms in this sector. As a result, the government has taken key steps in overhauling the geospatial ecosystem by liberalizing the geospatial guidelines, introducing a remote sensing policy and notifying the drone rules. With liberalized rules, the imagination and power of innovation inherent in our private enterprises can be unleashed.

Not stopping there, private participation has also been welcomed in the space sector. The Indian Space Research Organisation (ISRO) will share its well-developed infrastructure with private players and continue to focus on R&D. Technology developed by ISRO will also be transferred to private players through structured transfer of technology deals. The Indian National Space Promotion and Authorization Center (IN-SPACe) has been established as a single-window, independent nodal agency. The role

---

[9]"Applications Invited under the Design Linked Incentive (DLI) Scheme from Domestic Semiconductor Chip Design Firms', Press Information Bureau, 16 January 2022, https://bit.ly/3bUhYme, accessed on 8 July 2022.

of NewSpace India Limited has also been repurposed to become an aggregator for public demand and supplier of space services. It is expected that many opportunities for private participation will be opened through this move.

The future is likely to be characterized by increasing urbanization. Already, 11 per cent of the total global urban population resides in India. The UN estimates that in India, between 2018 and 2050, 416 million more people will be residing in urban areas.[10] What we must first achieve in this space is a rationalization and harmonization of the definition of an urban area. Consider the following: of the 7,933 urban settlements in India, 4,041 are classified as statutory towns with their own municipal corporations. The remaining 3,892 settlements are classified as census towns, which means that they meet the criteria for an urban settlement as per the *Census of India*. However, for administrative purposes, they remain classified as rural areas. They continue to be governed as villages. This system must evolve and be made uniform across India.

Ensuring sustainable urbanization will be key in delivering a higher standard of living for Indians. Planned urbanization will be a crucial pillar in this strategy. So far, much urban expansion has taken place in an unplanned manner, leading to poor living conditions and health outcomes. This planning, in turn, must happen around public transport, also known as transit-oriented development. This will be key in unlocking the agglomeration effects of urbanization and in combating the ill-effects of congestion. Urban planning must include public transport systems, such as bus rapid transit, light rapid transit, mass rapid transit and non-motorized transit systems.

---

[10]'68% of the world population projected to live in urban areas by 2050, says UN', Department of Economic and Social Affairs, United Nations, New York, 16 May 2018.

Relooking at floor space index (FSI, also known as Floor Area Ratio) norms will allow our cities to grow vertically, rather than going wide. For instance, the FSI in Singapore is 25, in Tokyo 20 and in New York, 15. Compare this to Mumbai, with an FSI of 1.3 and Delhi's of 3.5. The difference is clear. We must move away from creating urban sprawls by allowing higher FSIs. However, this move must be accompanied with scientific planning. The quality of roads, drainage and sewerage systems and water supply will have to be augmented considerably to grow vertically. Singapore is a fine example of having demonstrated that dense, vertical development can be complemented with biodiversity, greenery and liveability.

Ensuring adequate water availability and leveraging the principles of circular economy will be key to successful urbanization in India. Cities will be crucial in India's growth story going ahead. As is the norm now, private enterprise and the government must come together to devise innovative solutions in the design of urban spaces and in the delivery of urban services.

Seizing the Opportunity

The Asian growth experience has shown us that a transformation within a generation is entirely possible. However, India faces new challenges, which countries who grew earlier, did not. First, the developed countries of today (including those in Asia), grew through carbonizing their economies. Fossil fuels were burnt to the point that we are now facing a climate catastrophe.[11] India will

---

[11]'IPCC, 2021: Summary for Policymakers', *Climate Change 2021: The Physical Science Basis. Contribution of Working Group I to the Sixth Assessment Report of the Intergovernmental Panel on Climate Change*, (Masson-Delmotte, V., et al. [eds]), Cambridge University Press, Cambridge, United Kingdom and New York, NY, USA, pp. 3–32.

have to derive a growth model that does not rely on carbonization, as these countries have in the past. However, this also presents an opportunity for India to establish itself as a market leader in the green industrial transition. Second, digital technologies are proliferating like never before. The countries best able to leverage these technologies will be the most competitive in the future. Third, the global trade environment is likely going to be different to the environment in which the Asian countries grew. The multilateral trading order has been weakening, and countries are increasingly relying on bilateral agreements to drive trade and growth. Given these challenges in mind, the future avenues of growth must be seized upon by India to usher in our economic transformation.

The new economy that is emerging post-Covid-19 will be digital and green. We must ensure that Indian companies are at the forefront of this revolution. Industrial competitiveness will now be determined by green and digital processes. To carve out a share in GVCs, ensuring our competitiveness will be crucial. The world is increasingly demanding high-quality/high-technology products with a minimal carbon footprint. How do we ensure that such a transformation occurs? We must strive to make every Indian company go digital, green and lean. Manufacturing processes will have to be transformed, both in terms of digitizing and greening supply chains. This will certainly not be easy. But if there is one thing we have seen in this book, it is that we can never underestimate the passion, resilience and energy of Indian entrepreneurs. The start-up and innovation revolution that we have seen is also testament to this fact. Our young entrepreneurs and seasoned industry leaders must have the foresight and vision to drive change now and capitalize in the years ahead.

We must bring together technologies, such as IoT, cloud computing, big data analytics, smart manufacturing, AR-VR, robotics, machine-to-machine (M2M) communication and cyber security, to create digital factories of the future. Achieving such a change will require substantial investments in R&D, especially from private enterprise. This is one area where Indian firms and entrepreneurs have traditionally lagged behind. Even now, more global companies conduct R&D in India than domestic companies. For instance, India's R&D expenditure (as a percentage of GDP) stood at 0.6 per cent in 2018.[12] In contrast, South Korea's R&D expenditure stood at 4.5 per cent of GDP and China's at 2.1 per cent of GDP. Furthermore, the bulk of India's R&D comes from the public sector and not the private. This must change. If India's private sector does not start investing in commercial R&D, we will not achieve competitiveness in global markets.

Frontier technologies on which India can capitalize

1. **Primacy of AI**
   According to PricewaterhouseCoopers, AI has the potential to add $15.7 trillion to the global GDP by 2030, making it the largest commercial opportunity.[13] Use cases will cut across sectors and industries.

2. **Blockchain**
   Blockchain is another area with immense potential. Applications cut across areas such as traceability in agricultural produce, pendency in court cases and land registries, among others.

---

[12]The World Bank, World Development Indicators (WDI) Database, https://bit.ly/2XIV9sO, accessed on 8 July 2022.
[13]'Sizing the Prize: PwC's Global Artificial Intelligence Study—Exploiting the AI Revolution', PwC, https://pwc.to/3AWWXlr, accessed on 19 July 2022.

3. **AR-VR**

Connecting the physical and digital worlds, AR-VR creates integrated and immersive experiences. Augmented reality allows to project digital content in the physical world, whereas VR allows users to experience a new environment, using a range of senses. The applications are immense in areas such as defence and healthcare, among others.

4. **3D Manufacturing and printing**

The automation potential for certain kinds of manufacturing remains high. 3D manufacturing and printing will form the core of smart factories of the future, which will be digital and connected. India will need to build the capabilities of its workforce and invest in R&D to be at the forefront of the factories of the future.

5. **Drones**

Deliveries of consumer goods, crucial medical supplies in far-flung areas and assistance and relief in disaster-struck areas can be completely redefined through the use of drones. Apart from deliveries, drones can be game changers in surveying and mapping. Crop assessment, insurance estimation, fertilizer and pesticide spraying are just some examples in agriculture. Land surveying in urban and rural areas is another application. Drones will play an increasingly important role in national security as well.

The platform approach taken by the government so far must be extended to frontier technologies. Take the example of the JAM Trinity, the platform on which India's financial inclusion and tech-enabled service delivery is built. India Stack, with APIs such as Aadhaar authentication, eKYC, eSign and UPI, provide the backbone of India's direct benefit transfers and digital payments. Public digital infrastructure was effectively utilized by the private sector to build solutions. We must seek to replicate the success of this platform approach in upcoming digital technologies of the future and take our platform models across the world.

Technology has developed at breakneck speed. Many of the apps and devices that are now ubiquitous were not in existence 15–20 years ago. Social media, smartphones and cryptocurrencies are just some examples. It is hard to predict the direction in which technology may turn. Industry, academia and governments will have to come together to establish a framework to identify emerging technologies, rather than identifying technologies themselves. This framework could evaluate technologies based on their potential for job and wealth creation, and India's ability to become a world leader. This must also be a dynamic process, with technologies being continuously evaluated. The assumptions made in assessing the potential of technologies must also be validated through monitoring outcomes of these tech interventions.

At the same time, the framework must consider skilling requirements. Retaining the best of talent must be at the top of the agenda. Global partnerships and expertise must also be explored. Best practices from around the globe tell us an open innovation model, where the government buys and scales technologies from the private sector, has shaped the course of future tech. Take the example of Defence Advanced Research Projects Agency and National Aeronautics and Space Administration in the US. Research must also move from silos to a connected ecosystem. Digital literacy, digital infrastructure and internet penetration will be key to this future. India's education system will have to be realigned towards emphasizing skills-based education. The

NEP of 2020 is a step in this direction. Atal Innovation Mission is another. Workforce skills must consistently be upgraded to meet the technological challenges of the future. Learning how to learn will be the key skill.

There is also an opportunity afforded to companies by the upcoming upheaval. This new era we are entering will perhaps be one where businesses will be judged not just by profitability, but also their responsibility towards their workers and the environment. Research has shown that apart from investments, businesses benefit from several ways if they act in a responsible manner.[14] These businesses gain legitimacy, are able to secure government support, enhance their brand value, attract talent and win the trust of consumers. Further, building resilience and de-risking operations will be crucial to the health of businesses going forward.

The pandemic has also shown us that markets do not exist in isolation; they are only as strong as the underlying societies and natural environment in which they function. Investing in employees, focussing on employment conditions, social safety nets and access to health services, among others, are what talent is looking at in companies in this new world. To attract the best talent, companies must be prepared for these changes. Leaders will have to take a long-term view to transform their companies and operations. The companies that are able to best adapt to the new normal will thrive.

Seizing this opportunity will also require a rethinking of the role of the state, which must emerge as a facilitator of private investment and growth. This means that the state will also have to retreat from areas in which it has no business. Areas such

[14]Rajan, Mukund, and Col. Rajeev Kumar, *Outlast: How ESG Can Benefit Your Business,* Harper Business, New Delhi, 2021.

as mining, manufacturing and finance, among others, must entirely be private-sector driven. However, this does not mean that the state will recede; rather, its role will evolve, as history has shown us.

The countries that are most prosperous and provide the best quality of life for their citizens see both the private and public sectors coexist. Take the example of some of the leading countries in the World Bank's Ease of Doing Business Index in 2020: New Zealand (1), Denmark (4), South Korea (5), Norway (9) and Sweden (10). All of these countries have robust publicly funded health and education systems, and strong social security nets. Their strong response to the Covid-19 pandemic has also been documented. Social security and welfare schemes can only be sustainably financed through stable tax revenues which, in turn, can only accrue through a vibrant private sector. Economic growth and formalization of the economy will widen the tax net for both direct and indirect taxes.

Building our human capital and developing a pipeline of investible projects in physical infrastructure and tech-enabled service delivery must be the key domains of the state in the future. Technologies such as AI, cloud, blockchain, quantum computing, AR-VR and more can open up new possibilities for the government to deliver services to citizens in entirely new and more effective ways. To leverage such technologies, the state must consider utilizing open innovation models, such as Grand Challenges. In social sectors and service delivery, the government may consider becoming a buyer of emerging tech and innovation from Indian companies. Given the pace at which technology is expanding, new tools and analytics are increasingly available that can augment policymaking.

Public servants would, in turn, require a dynamic skill set. Lateral entrants hired at different levels can quickly augment capacities, especially specialized skills and knowledge. Governance needs to shift from focussing on tracking inputs and activities to tracking and delivering high-quality outcomes. Accountability and incentives to achieve priority national outcomes need to be built into the governance framework. To build strong accountability around outcomes, India needs to build a stronger data architecture to track outcomes. This would entail strengthening administrative data systems as well as conducting regular surveys to track progress on key outcomes. Through the data revolution, high-value data of public-sector interest is being generated by the private sector, social media and communities. Likewise, big data is generated through mobile phones, night lights, remote sensing, etc. Through data philanthropy and regulation, the state can leverage these non-conventional sources of data for deeper insights into policy making. First, access must be regulated through a robust framework, keeping in mind privacy and consent. Second, capabilities in data analytics must be built in the public sector to draw actionable insights from this data.

Several lessons emerge for India's young entrepreneurs and business leaders in navigating the new economy. First, tech adoption is a must. Second, be ready to take risks and venture into the unknown. Third, strive to be the best in the world, not just India. Fourth, fully leverage the economic opportunities offered by economic reforms. Fifth, pursue sunrise areas of growth. Sixth, establish links with start-ups and mainstream tech-based solutions across the supply chain. Finally, establish a brand that is defined by innovation and sustainability.

If we look back just 20 years, not many Indian entrepreneurs and companies found themselves at the summit of listings of the richest individuals or the biggest companies. India stands poised to establish itself as a dominant player in the emerging global economic order.

According to a recent report by Morgan Stanley, there are four trends shaping the global order: demographics, digitalization, deglobalization and decarbonization. India stands to benefit from all four. While the world is ageing, India is the youngest country in the world. India's public digital infrastructure has placed it favourably in the digital era, while other countries lag behind and are unprepared for the digital disruptions. While the world is resorting to protectionism, India is aligning itself with GVCs. Finally, India's strong commitment to climate action has made it a leader in the decarbonization space.

According to Morgan Stanley, the next decade is poised to be India's decade, with India becoming the third-largest economy by 2027, and the third-largest stock market by 2030.[15]

Achieving this will require both the public sector and the private enterprise to work together, in harmony. At the dawn of Independence, the public sector was expected to script India's growth story. However, 75 years after Independence, it is our young entrepreneurs, innovators and leaders who stand to lead us into a new era of growth and prosperity. The future looks exciting and India is poised to leapfrog technologically.

[15]'India's Impending Economic Boom', Morgan Stanley, 8 November 2022, https://mgstn.ly/3ZfvvZU, accessed on 2 January 2023.

INDEX